Like a PRO

Maple Tree Press Inc.
51 Front Street East, Suite 200, Toronto, Ontario M5E 1B3
www.mapletreepress.com

Distributed in Canada by Raincoast Books
9050 Shaughnessy Street, Vancouver, British Columbia V6P 6E5

Distributed in the United States by Publishers Group West
1700 Fourth Street, Berkeley, California 94710

Dedication
For Mom and Dad; for Michael and Andrew; and for Karl, of course!

Cataloguing in Publication Data
Becker, Helaine, 1961–
    Like a pro : 101 simple ways to do really important stuff / Helaine Becker ; Claudia Dávila.

ISBN 13: 978-1-897066-53-9 (bound) / ISBN 10: 1-897066-53-8 (bound)
ISBN 13: 978-1-897066-54-6 (pbk.) / ISBN 10: 1-897066-54-6 (pbk.)

1. Life skills—Handbooks, manuals, etc. 2. Young adults—Life skills guides. I. Dávila, Claudia II. Title.

HQ2037.B42 2006   646.7   C2005-904642-2

Design, art direction, & illustrations: Claudia Dávila

We acknowledge the financial support of the Canada Council for the Arts, the Ontario Arts
Council, the Government of Canada through the Book Publishing Industry Development
Program (BPIDP), and the Government of Ontario through the Ontario Media Development
Corporation's Book Initiative for our publishing activities.

ONTARIO ARTS COUNCIL
CONSEIL DES ARTS DE L'ONTARIO

Printed in Hong Kong

A   B   C   D   E   F

Like a PRO

101 Simple Ways to Do Really Important Stuff

WRITTEN BY
HELAINE BECKER

ILLUSTRATED BY
CLAUDIA DÁVILA

MAPLE
TREE
PRESS

CONTENTS

At Home

Anywhere and Everywhere

101 Things You've Just Just GOTTA Know

Let's face it, grown-ups have some pretty funny ideas about what's important. They say things like "Sit up straight" and "Clean your ears!" While no one will deny that grime-free ear canals are a bonus, there are other far more important life skills, don't you think? Like how to make an ace paper airplane or produce an ultra-loud whistle.

In the schoolyard, the surest route to success is knowing how to make the perfect snowball, blow a giant bubble, or pull off a mind-boggling magic trick. And who wouldn't want to master the art of roasting the perfect marshmallow, skipping a stone, or changing a bike tire?

If you're like a lot of other kids, you probably wouldn't mind learning how to deal with bullies, throw an awesome party, keep a secret, and be a good friend. And what about those practical skills that make getting on with the grown-up world easier—setting a table, making your bed, and scoring an A+ on a school project?

Wouldn't it be great to have all that how-to know-how right at your fingertips? Flip through this book and you'll find it all—and lots more! Let's get started with...

#1 HOW TO HAVE FUN!

To find out, just turn the page and read on...

SAY HELLO IN 10 DIFFERENT LANGUAGES

1 **Spanish** ☞ Hola (OH-la)

2 **Arabic** ☞ Al salaamu a'alaykum (Ahl sah-LAHMU ah ah-LAY-koom)

3 **Czech** ☞ Nazdar (NAH-zdar)

4 **French** ☞ Bonjour (bohn-ZHOOR)

5 **Hebrew** ☞ Shalom (Shah-LOHM)

6 **Hindi** ☞ Namaste (Nah-mah-STAY)

7 **Hungarian** ☞ Szia (ZEE-yah)

8 **Korean** ☞ Anyong haseyo (AN-yong HA-seh-yo)

9 **Swahili** ☞ Jambo (JAM-bo)

10 American Sign Language (ASL)

"Hello" is signed by moving the hand away from the forehead in a forward and downward motion, similar to a salute.

BRING ON THAT PESKY SNEEZE

Ahhh... ahhhh... ahhhh.... You know that annoying feeling when you're about to sneeze and it just won't happen? Here's a trick to bring it on and get it over with: Look up at the sun or another bright light. In a couple of seconds, your eyes will start to tear and ... *CHOO!!!!!!!!*

GET RID OF HICCUPS

1. Fill a glass with cold water.

2. Exhale, getting all the air out of your lungs.

3. Without inhaling, take ten sips of water. Slowly.

#4

4. When you've finished all ten sips, you may inhale (if you hiccup or breathe in during the process, start over).

5. Breathe a sigh of relief. Your hiccups are gone!

Beat the Jitters

Deal with a Bully

Boost Your Brain Power

At ScHOOL

Create a Website

Make a New Friend

How to Accept Your Oscar (You Never Know but Just in Case...)

Do an A+ Project

Sure, school means lots of challenges, but all you really need are a few easy-to-master skills. First things first: Use these tips to get out the door and arrive at your classroom—bright-eyed and bushy tailed, and with minutes to spare.

GET TO SCHOOL ON TIME

#5

WAKE UP!!!

Don't depend on parents or siblings to wake you—they may employ extremely **harsh tactics**. For example, siblings may shout in your ear and tear off your covers, leaving you in a shivering ball. Not a great start to the day!

If you don't have an **alarm clock**, get one. Learn how to set it so it rings at 7 a.m. (not during dinner at 7 p.m.). Turn it on. And make sure the volume is set REALLY LOUD.

Make **your lunch** the night before. Stack it neatly in the fridge. Then just put it in your lunchbox in the morning.

Lay out your clothes the night before. Make sure your clothes are clean and wrinkle free, so your folks don't send you back to change after you've dressed in the morning.

Put all your homework **in your backpack**, so it won't go missing or get left behind. Ditto for gym clothes, musical instruments, permission slips, and any library books.

LET'S MAKE A BET

Want to bet these tips will get you to school on time? Try following them for a week. Five bucks says they make a huge difference to how fast you get out the door in the morning. (Well, not a *real* five bucks, but try it anyway!)

Try getting into bed **a half-hour earlier** than normal. Feeling well-rested will make all the difference. (Turn the page for lots of smart tips on getting a great night's sleep.)

TELL LEFT FROM RIGHT

Too tired to get the right foot in the right shoe in the mornings? Need a surefire way to always remember your left and right? Hold up the back of both hands in front of you with your fingertips pointing straight up. Stick out your thumbs. Which hand makes an "L shape"? That's it—your left!

#6

13

GOOD

Here are some tricks you can use to sleep well, keep your nightmares at bay, and have sweet dreams all night long.

SLEEP TIGHT #7

Keep a dream journal to write down your dreams. Look for patterns. Say you have nightmares before an exam, then take extra care to get relaxed before bed on those nights. You can also use your dream journal to rewrite the ending of bad dreams to something less frightening.

Keep a healthy sleep routine. Try to go to bed at the same time every night, and get up at the same time—even on weekends.

Get plenty of exercise. You're more likely to sleep soundly if you are physically tired. Make sure you get in some good—preferably outdoor—activity every day.

NIGHTS

Talk about it. If something's on your mind that's bothering you, discuss it with a friend or a grown-up. Unhappy feelings or anxieties usually don't just go away. They pop up again in different ways—like in your nightmares.

Keep your door open. Even just a crack. This will help you remember that your family is close by. If you are scared, get up and find someone for reassurance, or a hug.

Avoid scary books or movies before bedtime. Sometimes, images from scary stories pop up in dreams—even two or three days after you've seen them.

Take a warm bath before bed. Relax and soak rather than doing something like playing a really exciting video game that will wind you up.

Avoid eating or exercising just before bedtime. Both these activities stimulate your system and make it tougher to get to sleep. Tossing and turning in a light doze might give you uneasy feelings that lead to nightmares.

Everybody's Worst Nightmares

Some of the most common nightmares include:

Your teeth are falling out.
You're in a car that's out of control.
Someone is chasing you.
You're falling.
You have a test and you haven't studied.
You're out in public—naked!

15

Even if you weren't born with the memory of an elephant, your powers of recall can be super-sized. Check out these tips to grow your own mega-memory.

BOOST YOUR BRAIN POWER

WORD GAMES

You have to **memorize** the names of the five Great Lakes by tomorrow. Don't panic! Try this watery word trick: Just think of the word "HOMES." That will give you the first letter of each name of the lakes: Huron, Ontario, Michigan, Erie, and Superior.

ROY G. BIV (said like a person's name) is another favorite **acronym**, which stands for the colors of the rainbow, in order: Red, Orange, Yellow, Green, Blue, Indigo, Violet.

i before e except after c
Say this rhyme to yourself to

A word like HOMES (above), made up of the first letters of several words, is called an acronym.

SIDE-SPLITTING SENTENCES

Another way to memorize a list of things or names is to create a funny sentence in which each word starts with the same letter as one of the words you need to remember:

For the 4 **oceans** (**I**ndian, **A**rctic, **A**tlantic, **P**acific): **I Am A Person.**

For the seven **continents** (**E**urope, **An**tarctica, **As**ia, **Af**rica, **A**ustralia, **N**orth America, **S**outh America): **Eat AN ASpirin AFter A Nighttime Snack.**

The phrase **M**y **V**ery **E**ager **M**other **J**ust **S**ent **U**s **N**ine **P**izzas corresponds to the **planets**, in order from the sun (**M**ercury, **V**enus, **E**arth, **M**ars, **J**upiter, **S**aturn, **U**ranus, **N**eptune, and **P**luto).

MORE WORD TRICKS

☞ Who runs your school? A principle or principal? To remember, think: Your principal is your PAL.

☞ Dessert or Desert? To remember that dessert has two "esses" and desert only one, just think you want two helpings of dessert.

☞ Be-lie-ve. To spell the word believe, remember it has the word "lie" in it.

☞ Spring ahead, fall back. Use this handy saying to remember which way to change your clocks for Daylight Savings Time.

remember how to spell words like chief or receiver.

*D*o numbers sometimes swim in your head just out of memory's reach? Try these tips to recall them.

RECALL NUMBERS

FIX UP A DATE

To remember dates, use **association**. For example, you could associate the date of your midterm exam, October 11, with Halloween, which you already know is on October 31. If you remember that the test is 20 days before Halloween, you can easily recall the exact date.

DATES = TIME & MONEY

Think of a date written as a **dollar figure** or a **time on a clock**. For example, the United States' Declaration of Independence was written in 1776. Picture the Declaration fitted out with a price tag of $17.76. Do you have a party to go to on December 15? Picture a digital clock wearing a party hat as it displays the time 12:15 (12th month, 15th day).

18

NEVER FORGET YOUR LOCK COMBINATION

Associate each number with an **animal**. Say, 43 gorillas, 7 penguins, and 16 fish. Picture the number of animals in your mind. Maybe have one of the 43 gorillas hold up a sign reading "43."

Write the numbers out a few times, then destroy the evidence.

Set the numbers to a funny **rhythm** or your favorite song.

Still having trouble recalling your lock combination? Try this **foolproof secret method**. Write the numbers down somewhere obvious, like on your binder, but disguise them as a phone number. Say, for example, your locker combination is 43-7-16. You would make up a person, such as "Grandpa at work," that your imaginary phone number belongs to. You would then write:

Grandpa at Work:
437-1600.

6th finger

$9 \times 6 =$ 54

LET YOUR FINGERS DO THE 9S

Use this "handy" trick to remember the 9 times table.

1 Hold your hands up in front of you, fingers pointing up.

2 If you are multiplying 9 x 6, fold down your sixth finger (counting always from the left). If it is 9 x 4, fold down the fourth finger, and so on.

3 How many fingers are standing up to the left of the folded finger? In this case (9 x 6), there will be five fingers (all the fingers on your left hand) standing up to the left of the folded sixth finger. These are your tens.

4 How many are standing to the right of the folded finger? In this case, four. These are your ones.

5 That's five in the tens, four in the ones. So 54 is the answer for 9 x 6.

Want an A+ every time? Follow these steps to success.

DO AN A+ PROJECT

#10

1. **Be clear on the requirements.** Make sure you know what form the project should take, what it needs to include, and exactly what your teacher will be grading it on.

2. **Choose a topic that interests you.** Also one on which you can find enough information. For example, it will be easier to find out about houses in Ancient Greece than how the Ancient Greeks felt about bugs.

3. **Do a little bit each day.** Work backwards from the project due date to plan when you will work on each step: Your research, building your model, or writing your cue cards.

4. **Do your research.** Collect information from books, Websites, and encyclopedias, taking notes as you work. And stay focused on your topic. If you are researching Ancient Greek houses, don't spend time reading or making notes on Greek medicine.

5. **Organize your information.** Make an outline. Divide your information on Greek houses into subtopics, such as building materials, room arrangements, roof design, and courtyard form and function.

6. **Get creative.** You have all your data. It's time to write the report, make the diorama, build your model, or paint your poster.

7 **Collect your materials.** Make sure you have everything you need to start work—like paper and enough printer toner to output your work, a shoebox for the diorama, clay for the model. Then go to work!

8 **Step back and look at what you've done.** When you've finished your first stab at the project, compare it to the project requirements. Is anything missing? What can you add to make it better? How is your spelling? Get a parent to look over your project as well. Then make any improvements.

9 **Do the Finishing Touches.** Of course, you did not leave all the work to the last minute, so all that's required on the night before your project is due is a final check. Make sure everything you need to hand in is included, and all required elements are present.

10 **Relax.** Your project is sure to be a success.

GO THE EXTRA MILE
Look to give your project that little bit more. A card with information about your diorama will impress the teacher. So would a Dictionary of Greek Housing Terms to accompany your house model.

DECIPHER ROMAN NUMERALS

#11

Reading the number **MMDCCLXVII** would have been no problem for someone in Ancient Rome. Can you decipher the number using the table below? (Answer on page 160.)

That was then...   *This is now...*

That was then...	This is now...
I	1
II	2
III	3
IV	4
V	5
VI	6
VII	7
VIII	8
IX	9
X	10
XX	20
XXX	30
XL	40
L	50
C	100
D	500
M	1000

MAKE AN AWESOME SPEECH

#12

You'll Need

cue cards

pen

research

trial audience

1. **Follow steps 1 to 5** for how to do an A+ project (page 20).

2. **Organize all your data on cue cards.** Write each main idea of your speech at the top of a cue card, then list the details below to support the idea.

3. **Put your cards in order.** Your first card should contain something grabby. A wacky but true statistic is always a good lead-in.

4. **Practice your performance.** A speech is really a show that you put on. You have to hold your audience with your voice, your manner, and riveting content.

5. **Rehearse in front of an audience.** Your parents, a friend, or a sibling will do. Listen to their feedback and their questions. Do you know the answers? If not, go back and do a little more research.

6. **Go through your speech several more times.** You want to know most of the content by heart so you're not reading off the cards. The cards are there just to jog your memory and keep your speech on track.

DID YOU KNOW THAT 99% OF COMMON HOUSE-HOLD DUST IS MADE UP OF DEAD SKIN? SO HOW DO WE STILL HAVE SO MUCH OF THE STUFF ON OUR BODIES? SKIN IS AMAZING STUFF....

Dr. Derma

7. **Hold the audience's attention.** Throw in some questions for them now and then. For example, "Do you know how long it takes for a new layer of skin to form?" Take guesses from the audience. Then tell them the correct answer.

8. **Command respect with your body language.** Stand straight; don't wiggle. Try to maintain eye contact with the members of the audience.

TIP

Take a deep breath to calm yourself before you begin your speech. Then just do what you practiced—you're bound to be a hit! (Turn the page for even more tips on keeping your cool in front of an audience.)

9. **Speak loudly and clearly, and slow down!** But don't deliver your speech like a zombie. Put animation into your voice. If you sound happy and excited by the information, your audience will catch your fever.

10. **Convey your emotions at times.** At an exciting part of the presentation, don't be afraid to wave your arm in emphasis, for example.

BEAT THE JITTERS

Does even the thought of being in front of an audience give you clammy palms? Showbiz pros suggest these pointers for overcoming stage fright.

1 **Know your environment.** Get to know the space beforehand. How big is the room? What's the audience size? How will they be seated? Also make sure you know how to use any equipment, like microphones or projectors.

2 **Relax.** If your throat muscles tighten up, your voice comes out squeaky. A dry mouth will also make speech difficult. Try "tricking" your body into relaxing by taking several deep breaths. Letting out a big breath tells your brain that everything is A-OK and you can feel calm.

3 **Breathe.** A lot of people actually forget to breathe normally when they are nervous! Plan places in your presentation to pause for a breath. And don't worry—the speech will seem to flow normally for your audience even if everything seems slow and strange to you.

4 **Remember: Your audience is on your side.** Your audience knows that getting up there is tough. Many of them suffer from stage fright too! They want to hear what you have to say, and are eager to enjoy your performance and see you succeed.

The scientific name for stage fright is glossophobia.

#13

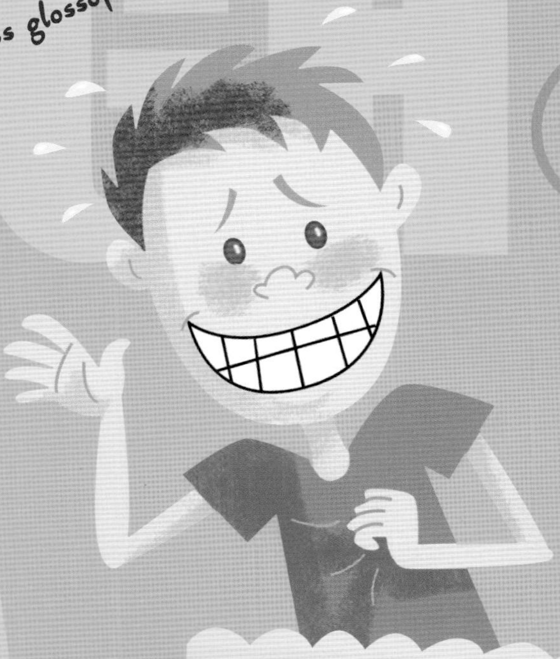

5 **Know your stuff.** The better prepared you are, the easier it will be to settle in and calm down once you get going. Unexpected questions won't fluster you—you know the answers.

6 **Enjoy yourself!** Once you are up there, expect the unexpected—that you will start to have fun. After all, how often do you have people hanging on your every word? Enjoy your time in the limelight!

TRY THIS

Just before you start, force a smile. The muscles in your face will tell your brain you are feeling happy.

Did you know?

Stage fright is the number one fear of most adults.

YOU NEVER KNOW

How to Accept Your Oscar

Daaahling, you've been nominated for an Academy Award. Of course you'll win—you're a star! So get ready for that trip down the red carpet.

Don't worry, Hollywood A-list types like you have "people" who take care of all the details so you can be perfectly polished. Here's your schedule.

THE DAY BEFORE

10:00 a.m. Massage, facial, pedicure, manicure until you're completely rubbery, soft, and smooth.

12:00 p.m. Lunch at exclusive restaurant. No pictures, please.

1:30 p.m. Watch your personal trainer swim your 60 laps in your Olympic-sized swimming pool. No need for a star like you to do all that work yourself.

3:00 p.m. Nap.

5:00 p.m. Fitting of marvelous outfit created by big-name designer. You look like a billion bucks.

8:00 p.m. Start liquid diet to trim off .0000001 ounces of unsightly flab.

8:05 p.m. End liquid diet. Switch to lobster diet.

10:00 p.m. Big day tomorrow. Early to bed with a magazine. It's all about your favorite star: You!

but just in case...

OSCAR DAY

12:00 p.m. Awaken from refreshing beauty sleep.

1:00 p.m. Dine on carrots and watercress.

2:00 p.m. Aromatherapy massage with hot oil.

3:30 p.m. Slip into outfit. Easy—you're drenched in oil!

4:00 p.m. Hair plastered into gravity-defying up-do.

4:30 p.m. Makeup application by someone fabulous.

5:30 p.m. Admire reflection one more time. Blow kisses to self in mirror.

6:00 p.m. Climb into limousine without creasing clothes for short ride to the ceremony. One last fix of hair, nails, bowties, and sunglasses for grand entrance.

7:00 p.m. Sashay down the red carpet. Wave to fans. Appear uncharacteristically gracious and sweet.

7:30 p.m. Red carpet interviews. Gush about how lucky you are, and wave to camera.

8:00 p.m. Take your seat. Practice expression of honest delight. Experience twinges of doubt, hunger.

9:00 p.m. Yes! They are calling your name! Bound gracefully to stage. Accept award. Smile, wipe away tear, and gush some more.

I CAN'T BELIEVE THIS! THANK YOU SO, SO MUCH, ALL OF YOU!

A SPECIAL THANKS TO THE ACADEMY, MY AGENT, MY MANAGER, MY DIRECTOR, THE MAKEUP LADY, MY TRAINER, MY MOTHER, MY DEAR DEPARTED

DOGGIE (I TOLD MYSELF I WOULDN'T CRY!), AND, OF COURSE, ALL OF YOU WONDERFUL FANS.

Sure, friendship sometimes takes work. But isn't it worth it? Here's everything you need to know to be there for your friend when he or she needs you.

BE A GREAT FRIEND

#15

Top 10 Friendship Rules

1. Treat your friend the way you want to be treated.
2. Keep secrets that are told to you.
3. Keep your promises.
4. Share things with your friend.
5. Tell your friend the truth.
6. Stick up for your friend.
7. Take turns.
8. Be there when your friend needs you.
9. Forgive. We all make mistakes.
10. Have fun with your friend!

Buddy Bonding

Shine Together: Buy two inexpensive pairs of earrings, say, a pair of moons and a pair of suns. Switch the earrings so each pair has a sun and moon. Give one set to your pal, and wear the matching pair yourself!

Cheer Together: Find a sports team you both like. Plan to cheer them on together when they play. You can also each choose a fave player and call each other by that player's name or nickname.

Give 'em a **hug** and show 'em that you really care.

Listen as he describes his problem. If he asks for advice, you can offer it. If not, don't. Just sympathize with his plight.

Paint her a picture of something that you know she likes. Frame it and give it to her as a **cheer-up gift**.

Take your friend out for some **fun**! Going bowling or taking a bike ride can do wonders to lift someone's spirits.

Ask him to help you with a problem of your own! Taking his mind off his worries will help. So will the feeling that he is **useful** to someone else.

How to Cheer Up a Friend

Call just to let him know you are thinking about him.

Bake her her favorite cake or most adored kind of cookies.

Find a **picture** of both of you together. Frame it and give it to him.

Make a collection of really funny comics or cartoons. Give it to him to make him **laugh**.

Is she unhappy because she got a bad mark on a test? Offer to **help** her study for the next one.

Make a pair of **friendship bracelets**. Give one to her. Wear the other one yourself.

Your friend has just spilled the beans. She has told you a very top-secret secret. The first thing you need to ask yourself is, should you keep it?

#16

KEEP A SECRET

Most of the time, you should keep your friend's secret. It is one of the top 10 rules for friendship, after all. No one wants a friend they can't trust. But sometimes secrets can hurt people. **You should never keep secrets about something that might be dangerous or may cause harm.** Trust your instincts. Can you tell a good secret from a bad one? Take this quiz to find out. Decide which secrets you should keep and which ones you should tell your mom or dad about ASAP! Check your answers on page 160.

1 Your pal is planning a surprise party for his dad.

2 Your friend confesses that she hates broccoli.

3 Your best bud confides that his brother is thinking of joining a gang.

4 Your friend's father tells you not to tell your parents about the time he drove you home from school.

5 Your chum is arranging to meet, in person, a boy she met online.

6 Your friend tells you that he is seriously thinking of running away from home.

7 Your friend likes another kid in the class. You know, a lot.

Zip Your Lips

Once you have decided that your friend's secret is neither dangerous nor hurtful, you MUST keep it! But, let's face it, it's hard to keep mum about juicy news! Try these suggestions:

Think about **how you would feel** if your friend told the whole school you still have a stuffed rabbit named Mrs. Bunnyslippers. Every time you consider blabbing, just picture it happening.

When you are with other friends who are **gossiping**, resist the temptation to join in. True friends will admire your restraint.

Exchange **friend-ship bracelets** with your friend. Wear yours. Every time you think about betraying her secret, take a look at the bracelet. Would you really want to lose her as a friend?

Still don't trust yourself? **Tell your friend a secret, too!** Then if you tell his secret, you'll know that he could tell yours!

An old tradition says that our tongues are such a dangerous weapon they are stored behind two strong gates—our lips and our teeth. Picture locking your gates and **throwing away the key**.

OOPS!

#17

SAY SORRY

You lost your friend's favorite jacket that he lent you last Tuesday. Skip the excuses. Follow these no-nonsense steps to say you're sorry.

1. Own up right away. Say, "I'm really sorry, but I left your jacket on the bus by accident."

2. You will also have to make good—either by buying another jacket just like it, or giving him the money so he can replace it.

3. If he gets angry, don't get angry at him in return. It's natural for him to be mad that you were careless, but he should cool down and appreciate that you've been honest with him and that you want to make amends.

31

*I*t's actually pretty easy. You meet 'em, greet 'em, then need 'em.

#18 MAKE A NEW FRIEND

Did you meet someone new that you think might be a great friend? The first step is simple. **Introduce yourself**. Just go up and say, "My name's Camilla. I saw you in French class the other day. You're new to the school, right?" Your new classmate will be so happy you made the first step, you're three-quarters of the way home.

SHAKE HANDS

Make a positive impression when you meet someone more formally, or receive an award.

1 Remove your gloves, if you are wearing any. (Cold weather exception: If it's twenty below, you can leave them on, but say, "Excuse my glove!")

2 If your hands are sweaty, try and dry them off without anyone noticing before you shake.

3 Extend your right hand with your thumb pointing to the ceiling.

4 Grasp the other person's hand firmly. No wet-noodle fingers, please, and no knuckle-rubbing squeezes either!

5 Look the other person right in the eye.

6 Pump the other person's hand up and down once, twice, three times.

7 Then let go!

#19

Ask questions. Find out a little about your new classmate. You're sure to discover a few things you have in common.

Be yourself. You should never pretend to be something you're not, or to like things that you really don't like, just to make someone like you. Real friends accept you as you are.

Invite your potential new friend to an activity in which **she can be the "star."** If you know, for example, that the new girl, Miranda, is a great soccer player, ask her to show you some of her skills. She'll be happy that you're interested in something that is important to her too.

As you get to know each other, ask yourself whether your new friend **shares the same values** as you. For example, is she honest, reliable, and kind? Great! If not, don't feel bad to let this maybe-a-friendship slide. Choose to *stay* friends only with other kids who think and behave the way you like to.

Even pros need to take a break. When you need to rest your weary brain from all your academic pursuits, why not take a break with these simple pleasures.

#20 DRAW A CARTOON DOG

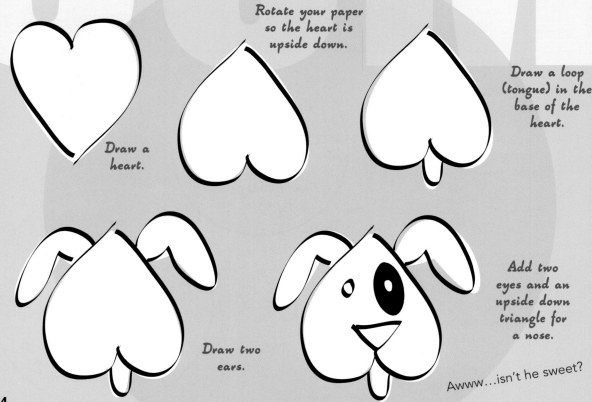

Draw a heart.

Rotate your paper so the heart is upside down.

Draw a loop (tongue) in the base of the heart.

Draw two ears.

Add two eyes and an upside down triangle for a nose.

Awww…isn't he sweet?

WIN A STARING CONTEST

There is a simple trick: Don't actually look at the other player's eyes. Look between them, or slightly above them. Relax your eyes and let them go slightly out of focus. Then think of something other than what you are doing. Relax, breathe deeply, and win!

#21

35

Is school a nightmare because someone is bullying you? Do you wake up every morning feeling sick at the thought of you-know-who? Don't take bullying lying down.

DEAL WITH A BULLY #22

Enter the bullring with these tricks of the matador's trade and grab that bully by the horns.

TELL SOMEBODY

Being bullied is nothing to be ashamed of. Tell a friend, parent, caregiver, or teacher. Sharing your secret will be a big relief, and they may be able to do something to nip the bullying in the bud. And chances are the person you tell will have had a bullying experience, too, and will be able to give you good advice.

BE KIND TO YOURSELF

The bully is busy trying to bring you down. Don't help him out by ragging on yourself or thinking things like, "There must be something wrong with me for this to be happening." No way! It's the bully who has the real problem. Remind yourself what a wonderful person you are.

BELIEVE IN YOURSELF

Have confidence that you can deal with a bully in an effective, peaceful manner.

DEFUSE THE BULLY

Most bullies have low self-esteem. Sometimes you can turn a bully into an ordinary kid by being generous and kind. For example, is the bully struggling with schoolwork? Ask her if you can help her out. Or invite her to join you and your friends at lunch.

WALK AWAY

Most bullies get a charge out of watching you suffer. Don't give them the satisfaction. Just turn around and leave.

STAND UP FOR YOURSELF

There's no reason to do what a bully says, or to let him walk all over you. If someone starts pushing you around, square your shoulders, look him dead in the eye, and say in a loud, firm voice, "STOP DOING THAT!" Chances are he'll stop in his tracks and recognize that you won't be put down.

TELL THE BULLY HOW YOU FEEL

Use powerful "I" statements. "I don't like it when you talk to me like that. I deserve to be treated with respect, just like you." If the bully responds by belittling you don't react by getting upset. Tell her how you feel again, with conviction.

JOIN WITH OTHER FRIENDS

Bullies choose people who seem vulnerable. They hardly ever pick on people in a group. Form an alliance with other kids. When you see a bully approach, join together. If no other kids are in sight, look for a teacher or other adult to help you out if you need it.

If you try all of these tactics and the bully won't quit or you are afraid he or she may hurt you physically, get help from an adult immediately.

BULLIES CLOSE-UP

Why Kids Become Bullies

While there are many differences among them, bullies share certain traits. Often they are unhappy, and many struggle in school. Many bullies have poor social skills. They don't know how to make friends and can't read the social signals the rest of us take for granted. They get angry, and fight back the only way they know how.

A Pack of Bullies

This is the worst type of bullying. Kids who would never bully other kids alone gather strength when they are part of a group. You must talk to a grown-up when this kind of bullying is happening.

What can YOU do?

Of course, you should never put yourself in danger, but you can act to stop others from being bullied. Here's how:

• **Act up.** Go over to the victim and join forces with her or him. Most bullies won't want to take on the two of you.

• **Speak up.** Imagine that one of your classmates tells all of you not to play with someone...or else. Tell her you'll be friends with whomever you want.

Need a fast and painless way to make up fair teams or choose someone to be "It?" Try these fun ways kids have invented to get games off to a good start.

#23 CHOOSE "IT" AND MAKE TEAMS

CHANT IT OUT

1. These chanting rhymes work best for group games.

2. Players should stand in a circle and each put a fist in the middle.

3. Invite the player whose ball it is, or who has the longest name, to chant one of the following rhymes and count off the other players.

4. The chanter recites the rhyme, touching each fist once as he says each word.

5. The player who is touched on the last word of the chant then becomes "It" or is eliminated. If she is eliminated, repeat the chant and keep eliminating players until only one remains—It.

6. To form teams, the first player selected goes to team A, the second to team B, and so on.

One Potato, Two Potato

One potato, two potato, three potato, four.
Five potato, six potato, seven potato, more.

Bubblegum

Bubblegum bubblegum in a dish
How many pieces do you wish?
The person, who is touched on the word "wish," chooses a number, say 6. The chanter then counts up to six, going around the circle, touching one fist on each number. The sixth person is "It" or "Out."

Icka Bicka

Icka bicka soda cracker
Icka bicka boo;
Icka bicka soda cracker
Out goes Y-O-U!

WHO GOES FIRST?

When your game has only two players or teams,
try one of these methods for choosing who goes first.

You'll Need
a baseball bat

Batter Up

1. A neutral person holds a bat vertically, handle end up.

2. He/she tosses the bat lightly, straight up in the air, then catches it anywhere along its length.

3. A player from team A grasps the bat with her hand right above the first person's—touching hands.

4. A player from team B then places his hand right above Player A's hand.

5. Player A puts her other hand above Player B's hand. Then Player B's hand is next. Repeat until someone's hand reaches the knob at the top of the bat.

6. That player's team goes first.

Odds or Evens

1. Two players bunch one of their hands into a fist.

2. One player chooses "Odds." The other then becomes "Evens."

3. Together, they chant, "One, two, three, go!"

4. On "go," each player puts out either one finger (the pointer) or two fingers (pointer and middle finger).

5. Count the total number of fingers (two, three, or four). If the total is an even number, Evens goes first. If it is odd, Odds goes first.

CREATE A WEBSITE

So, you want to have your very own Website. Don't touch the computer yet—the first step requires good old-fashioned pencil and paper.

Title: Guinea Pigs Take Over the World

I. Raising Guinea Pigs
(Guinea Pigs Take over the World!)

A. My six prizewinning guinea pigs (names and pics)

1. Fluffmeister
a. where I got him
b. what he likes to do

2. Dinglebones
a. where I got him
b. what he likes to do

3. Prince Charmant
a. where I got him
b. what he likes to do

4. Snappy
a. where I got her
b. what she likes to do

5. Snoopy
a. where I got her
b. what she likes to do

6. Wendell
a. where I got him
b. what he likes to do

II. Care and Feeding of Guinea Pigs
A. What They Like to Eat
B. How to Clean the Cage
C. Guinea Pig Breeding

TIP
If your word processing program allows for "smart," or "curly," quotes, turn them off. They will show up on your page as weird icons—not quotation marks.

Step 1:
Choose Your Message

• Decide what you want your page to be about. Do you want it to describe your hobbies, your favorite sport or hometown team, your own athletic career, your favorite music group, or a great project you did for the environment?

• Sketch out what your page or pages will look like. Leave places for a title, some pictures, and your text.

Step 2:
Create Your Text

• Write an outline (see left)—a plan listing the important points you want to cover. Use headings and subheadings to organize the information. Then create a page or paragraph of your Website for each section, topic, or subtopic of your outline.

• Start with an attention-grabbing title, like "Guinea Pigs Take Over the World!" Add an introduction to tell viewers what your page is about.

• Break your text into manageable chunks. Your page will be a lot easier to read—and snazzier to look at—if you put in frequent paragraph breaks and horizontal rules. Also think about where it would make sense to insert pictures or illustrations.

• Use a word processing program to create your text documents for each part of your outline. Save each document with a name ending with ".htm" (or ".html" if you are using a Macintosh). For example, a document describing your pet guinea pig would be called Fluffmeister.htm" or "Fluffmeister.html."

• Save all the documents as "Text Only."

Step 3:
Format Your Text for the Web

• To make your Web page look nice, you have to format it.

• Internet browsers look for instructional tags in your text that tell them how to arrange your words and pics on the screen. The tags are part of a computer language (see HTML Dictionary, page 42).

• You will have to insert the tags into your text document. Each tag begins with a "less than" (<) symbol and ends with a "greater than" (>) symbol.

• Tags often come in pairs. The first tag is written "plain" <title>, while the second in the pair includes a slash mark </title>. These paired instructions tell where each type of formatting begins and where it ends. For example, you start your document with <html> and end it with </html>.

41

HTML DICTIONARY

Check out some common HTML (HyperText Markup Language) tags.

• <title>...</title> Use these tags so your title will appear at the top of the browser window.

• <h1>...</h1> header, level 1. Insert these tags to create a header, such as **Meet My Prize-winning Guinea Pigs!** or **Care and Feeding**.

• <h2>...</h2> Use these tags to create subheads underneath each topic. For example, under **Care and Feeding**, is **How to Clean the Cage**. Use the outline you made in step 2 to help decide where to put your headers and subheads.

• <body>...</body> Use these tags to set off your main text.

This is the marked-up text, as you would enter it into your text document.

<h1> Meet My Prizewinning Guinea Pigs! </h1>

<h2> Fluffmeister </h2>

<body>Fluffmeister was the first guinea pig I ever owned. He was given to me by my neighbor, Miss Papplethwaite. Fluffmeister is white and gold, with a brown patch on his left ear. </body>

<h2>Snappy</h2>

<body> Some people don't think guinea pigs have much personality. They never met Snappy! Snappy likes to play with balls. She also likes to crawl into your pocket and snuggle there.</body>

This is how it's going to look on the Web page.

Meet My Prizewinning Guinea Pigs!
Fluffmeister

Fluffmeister was the first guinea pig I ever owned. He was given to me by my neighbor, Miss Papplethwaite. Fluffmeister is white and gold, with a brown patch on his left ear.

Snappy

Some people don't think guinea pigs have much personality. They never met Snappy! Snappy likes to play with balls. She also likes to crawl into your pocket and snuggle there.

Step 4:
Add Pictures

Do you have some awesome digital photos of Fluffmeister? Use the image command <img src="imagename.gif"> or <img source="imagename.jpg"> to insert them. Make sure a copy of the picture is in the same folder as your document. You can also download some images from other Websites. Do not download copyrighted images; only use images that are free for use. Check the source Website for this information.

The Wonderful World of
Guinea Pigs

Thanks for visiting my Website all about my favorite pet: guinea pigs! Click on the links at the right to read more...

A Day in the Life

See Photos

Raising Guinea Pigs

More Info

TIP

Want a more detailed look at the HTML tags? While you're surfing the Net, go to the "View" menu in your Internet browser and select "Page Source" or "View Source." Then you will be able to see the source text document for the page that includes the HTML tags. By comparing the Web page to the source document, you will see instantly how each command works.

Step 5:
Getting Your Page Online

Wouldn't it be nice if the whole world could see your finished masterpiece? You'll need to open an account with an Internet Service Provider (ISP) to put it up on the Web. The ISP you use for your own Web access may have a service that will allow you to put up your Website for free. If not, you can find services available on the Web that will. When your site is up and running, give its URL, or Web address, to your friends and family so they can see your efforts online!

SURF SAFELY #25

Ride the waves of these tips to surf the Internet safely.

Do not give out **personal information**, such as your address or telephone number, or the name and location of your school. Really bad people can get hold of this information.

If you come across any information that makes you feel **uncomfortable**, tell your parents ASAP.

Never agree to **get together** with someone you have "met" online. Check with your parents first. If they agree to a meeting, make sure the meeting is in a public place and one of your parents goes with you.

Never send anyone **your picture**—or anything else personal—without first checking with your parents or a school advisor.

Do not do anything that **hurts others** or is against the law. For example, it is illegal to use material that is copyrighted (pictures, text, or music) without permission, to issue threats, or to publicly say or write anything untrue about another person.

Talk with your family to set up family rules for using the Internet. The family rules should cover when you are allowed to go online, for how long, and what sites or areas are OK to visit. Then stick to the rules—they are for your own safety!

Do not say anything to anyone via text messaging or email that you would not say directly to his or her face.

Do not respond to messages that are mean or ones that make you feel uncomfortable. It is not your fault if you are sent a message like that.

Don't give out your **Internet passwords** to anyone—except your parents or guardian.

If you receive a **hurtful message**, tell your parents right away. They can contact your service provider and put an end to the messages.

Skip a Stone

OUT
and

How to Survive on a Desert Island
(You Never Know but
Just in Case...)

Spin a Basketball on Your Finger

Plant a Flower

Find the Big Dipper

ABOUT

Throw a Frisbee

Fly a Kite

FLY A KITE

Rule the skies with these high-flying kite tips.

Diamond Kite

Delta Kite

Parafoil Kite

first things first...

Different kites fly better in different conditions. Look below for the best type to use to suit your flying conditions.

LIGHT TO MEDIUM WIND:
(8–24 km / 5–15 mi. per hour winds) use a delta, diamond, or dragon kite

MEDIUM TO STRONG WIND:
(13–40 km / 8–25 mi. per hour winds) use a box or stickless parafoil

Choose a day with steady wind—that means you can see leaves moving in the trees but it's not gusty or too calm. NEVER fly a kite in rain or lightning.

Grab a friend. It's easier to get the kite off the ground with a helper—and it's more fun with two.

Choose the right spot. Parks and beaches are ideal. Select a clear, open area, away from roads, power lines, and trees (a.k.a. "kite eaters!").

Check your kite before you fly to make sure nothing is tangled, torn, or loose.

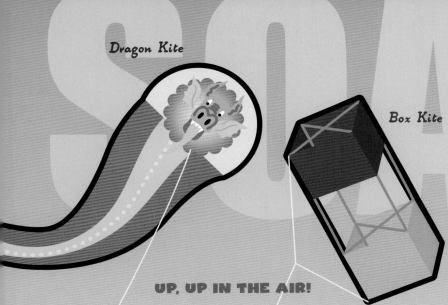

Dragon Kite

Box Kite

UP, UP IN THE AIR!

1 You've got the right kite, the right weather conditions, and the right launchsite. To begin, stand with your back to the wind. Hold your kite up by the bridle point—the part where the kite attaches to the string on your reel.

2 Let some line out. If there is enough wind, your kite will lift off.

3 Not enough wind for this technique? Have your pal walk about ten steps downwind and hold the kite up over her head. Shout "NOW!" Your friend should let the kite go. At the same time, you start pulling on the kite line.

Try using a hand-over-hand technique. You might run a few steps away from your friend, until the kite gains altitude.

4 Let the kite fly out a little bit. Isn't it pretty? Gently tug on the line. This will help tip the kite so it will climb. Repeat a few times, gradually letting out line and tugging on it to make it go higher.

5 Cool! Your kite is really up there! Let out enough line until your kite has found a good altitude where there is a steady breeze. Enjoy! Don't forget to let your friend have a turn.

KITE CALAMITY TROUBLESHOOTING

The kite keeps sinking, tail first. Not enough wind—fuhgeddaboutit. Go home and eat a popsicle instead.

The kite keeps sinking, head first, or spins. Too much wind. Try a different type of kite, try adding a tail to keep it more stable, or go home and fix yourself a hot chocolate.

The kite got stuck in a tree. Congratulations! You are now an official kite-flyer. Go home, enjoy a popsicle AND a hot chocolate. If you're lucky, your kite will come down on its own before you turn 21.

How does your garden grow?
Better with this green-thumb gardening know-how right at your fingertips.

PLANT A SEED

#27

You'll Need

10 cm (4 in.) plastic pot with drainage holes in the bottom

plastic saucer

potting soil

small garden trowel

sunflower seeds (garden varieties—not salted snack varieties!)

watering can

water

1. Place the saucer under the pot.
2. Using the trowel, fill the pot about halfway up with potting soil.
3. Place a few (6–8) seeds into the soil. The seeds should not touch each other.
4. Cover the seeds with soil. Gently press the soil down with your finger.
5. Water lightly to dampen the soil. You've watered enough when a few drips leak out from the bottom of the pot.
6. Check the pot daily. When the soil becomes dry, water again—but not too much.
7. In a few days, you might see the seed sprouts starting to poke through the soil. Keep the soil moist but not soggy.
8. In a few more days, you may see the first pair of leaves on several of the sprouts. Once a few pairs of leaves have formed, select the seedlings of two or three of the strongest and tallest looking plants. Keep those but pull out all the others to make room for the strongest ones to grow. Pull gently—so you don't pull out the whole lot by accident.
9. If the soil outside is completely warm and there is no more danger of frost, you can transplant your seedlings to the garden. Just follow the steps in "Plant a Flower" (right).

50

#28 PLANT A FLOWER

You'll Need

watering can

water

flower seedling

root starter
(root-stimulating
hormone, available at
gardening stores)

trowel

compost or
rotted manure
(available from
gardening stores)

1. Fill a watering can with water. If the soil in your seedling's container is hard and dry, water to soften it a bit.

2. Then add root starter to the water in the watering can. Check the package for how to use, and how much to use—it depends on the amount of water your watering can holds.

3. Choose a site for your flower. Does it require full sun, part sun, or shade? The tag that comes with the seedling will tell you.

4. Using your trowel, dig a hole twice as deep and twice as wide as the seedling's container. Loosen up the dirt remaining in the hole so it is crumbly and soft—better for tender new roots to grow into.

5. Add a trowelful of compost or manure to the hole. Mix it with the soil. The bottom third to half of the hole should now be filled with a soft, rich soil mixture.

6. Turn the seedling container onto its side. Squeeze the container to release the seedling and soil. If there are two or more seedlings, gently pull them apart so that each seedling has an equal number of roots. Keep as much of the soil with the roots as possible.

7. Set one seedling, along with its dirt, into the hole, lightly pressing the root ball down into the loose soil so the top of the root ball is just below ground level. Cover the root with a bit of soil and water.

8. Refill the rest of the hole with the dirt you dug out of it. Press down with your hands to compact the soil around the seedling.

9. Water the seedling generously. This will help firm the plant in the ground, get rid of air pockets in the soil, and nourish the seedling. Over the next days and weeks, make sure that the soil around your seedling remains moist, but not soggy. Enjoy your beautiful garden!

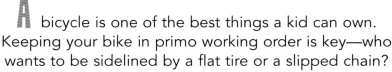
A bicycle is one of the best things a kid can own. Keeping your bike in primo working order is key—who wants to be sidelined by a flat tire or a slipped chain?

CHANGE A BIKE TIRE

STEP 1: *Remove the Tire from the Wheel Rim*

You'll Need

3 tire levers

bicycle pump

1. Take the whole wheel off the bike. Some bikes have a quick release mechanism. Others will require a wrench or pliers to remove the bolt.

2. If the tire is not completely flat, let out any remaining air by pressing on the air valve nib.

3. Insert the narrow end of a tire lever between the tire and the rim. Pull the lever down, clipping the hook end to the nearest spoke.

4. Slide your hands around the wheel, about two spokes along.

5. Repeat steps 3 and 4 with the second tire lever.

6. Repeat steps 3 and 4 with the third lever.

7. Take the first lever out. Slide over two spokes from the third lever, and repeat steps 3 and 4 again, using the lever you just removed.

8. Continue around the wheel, inserting and removing levers, until one side of the tire is free of the rim. It should be easy now to pull the whole tire off the rim with your hands.

STEP 2: *Change the Inner Tube*

1. Pull the old tube out of the tire. If you intend to reuse it, set it aside to patch up later.

2. Run your hand around the inside of the tire to see if you can find what caused the flat. **Be very careful!** If it was a nail or shard of glass, it could cut your finger just the way it cut your inner tube. If you find any foreign objects, remove them. Check the outside of the tire again to make sure nothing is stuck.

3. With a bicycle pump, pump a bit of air (one or two pumps) into the new tube. Then slide the new tube into the tire.

STEP 3: *Put the Tire Back onto the Wheel Rim*

1. Push the air valve on the inner tube through the hole in the wheel rim.

2. Now use your fingers to work your way around the wheel to slip one whole side of the tire onto the wheel rim. Check that the inner tube is not getting pinched between the tire and the rim. If it is, gently pull it out from the other side.

3. Turn the wheel and continue to push the rest of the tire onto the rim with your thumbs. When the tire is nearly all on, it will become very tight. Take a deep breath and give it one last hard push with both thumbs. You got it!

4. Reinflate the tire and reattach the wheel to the bike frame. You're ready to ride!

HELMET HOW-TO

Pros know that wearing a well-fitted bike helmet is a must. The front of the helmet should cover your forehead. Make sure the strap is fastened properly around your chin—not too tight or too loose. Your ears should fit inside the "Y" of each strap.

REPLACE A BIKE CHAIN

1. Uh-oh, you've slipped your chain. No big deal. Stop pedaling as this may wedge the chain between the gears and the frame, making it really tough to remove. Steer yourself out of traffic and into a safe location, and dismount.

2. Steady the bike by leaning it up against a rail or post. Use the kickstand if you have one.

derailleur

3. Most chains tend to slip off in front, off the large gears. With your left hand, push the derailleur (the knobby bit at the back of the chain path) forward slightly. This will put some slack into the chain, so you can move it.

4. Use your right hand to put the chain back in place on the front chain ring. Release the derailleur.

5. If everything looks like it's in place, get on your bike. Pedal backward first to make sure everything is working.

6. Clean off your hands after this mucky job. Greasy handlebars can be dangerous if they make your hands slip while you're trying to steer. If you are near a grassy area, wipe your hands on the grass. Or wipe them on the sidewalk and rub a little dirt on them. Once at home, wipe as much grease off of your hands as possible with an old rag or a paper towel, then scrub with soap and water.

TIP: Sometimes chains slip off because they are too dry. Keep your bike in the best working order by regularly oiling your chain and keeping it lubricated. A well-oiled gear train will also be protected from rust and dirt.

USE CYCLING SIGNALS

Use these hand signals to communicate with drivers, other bikers, and pedestrians for a safe and enjoyable ride.

STOP

Hold your left arm out to your side and bend at the elbow so your palm is facing the rear, and fingers are pointing toward the ground. Use this same signal if you are slowing down quickly.

LEFT TURN

Hold your left arm straight out at your left side—as if you were pointing to the left (you can even point if you like).

RIGHT TURN

There are two accepted signals:

1. Point your right arm straight out to your right side, as if you were pointing to the right (point your finger, if you like).

2. Hold your left arm out to your left side, bending at your elbow so your palm is facing forward and your fingers pointing up.

Speak Up!

Hand signals are great for communicating your intentions. So is your mouth. Don't be afraid to add your voice to your hand signals.

"TURNING LEFT!"

"TURNING RIGHT!"

"SLOWING DOWN!"

"STOPPING!"

"PASSING ON YOUR LEFT!"
(when you're overtaking a slower rider in front of you)

Get the most out of those long days of summer with these hot tips.

#32 SKIP A STONE

1 Choose the right stone: one that's nice and flat, even in thickness, and about the size of your palm. It should weigh no more than a ball you can comfortably throw, such as a tennis ball.

2 Hold the stone between your thumb and middle finger, with your thumb on top. Hook your index finger along the stone's edge.

3 Stand facing the water at a slight angle so that the foot on the side of your throwing arm is a bit further back. Bend your knees slightly.

4 Bend your wrist back fully. Release the stone out in front of you and down at the same time, with a sharp snap of the wrist to give it some spin. The faster the better. The lower your hand is at the release (that is, closer to the surface of the water) the better your stone will skip. When the stone hits the water, it should be almost completely parallel to the water's surface.

5 Plink! Plink! Plink! Plink! Don't forget to count the number of skips.

Did you know?

French scientists actually built a robot to test for the best stone-skipping method! They discovered that the greatest number of skips come from 10 cm (4 in.) long stones thrown at 96 km (60 mi.) per hour, at an angle of exactly 10°. Now that's science!

GIVE A PRIMO PIGGYBACK RIDE

#33

For giving a little kid a piggyback ride:

1 Get down on all fours, on your hands and knees.

2 Instruct your young friend to climb on. They should hold on at your shoulders.

3 Crawl forward. Neigh as desired.

For giving an older kid a piggyback ride:

1 Squat down, and lean forward. Rest your weight on your hands, if necessary.

2 Have your friend lean on your back. His hands should be clutching your shoulders, not wrapped around your (Aggh!) neck.

3 Using all the strength in your legs and arms, push yourself up to standing position. Lift your rider at the same time. They should now wrap their legs around your waist.

4 Jiggle your passenger a bit, just for fun, and to help adjust their position for your comfort. Then walk or trot to give 'em an exciting ride.

BE SUN SMART

#34

Unless you're a vampire, chances are you will spend time outside in the sun. Here's how to avoid a painful sunburn.

Cover up with a sun hat, and ideally a long sleeve shirt and pants.

Use a good-quality sunblock to cover all exposed areas of your skin. If you will be swimming, choose one that is waterproof. Reapply as directed on the package.

Wear sunglasses with UV (ultraviolet) protection, especially near water or in snowy conditions, since water and snow reflect large amounts of burning rays.

YOU NEVER KNOW

How to Survive on a Desert Island

#35

A word of advice: memorize these tips because there's a pretty good chance you won't have this book with you if you ever get left behind to fend for yourself on a deserted desert island!

1 First order of business: find a source of fresh water—pronto. Seawater's no good. All that salt will dehydrate you even more.

2 Congratulations, you found a bubbly freshwater spring behind a coconut tree! That coconut tree's going to come in handy, too. If you can smash a coconut open on a rock, voilà—you've got a water scoop, a drinking cup, plus a sweet coconut snack.

but just in case...

3 Time to make some shelter. Think: snug and leafy to keep you warm at night and out of the sun by day.

4 Build yourself a raised bed under the shelter. It's not so much the big beasts you need to worry about here but the wee ones, like ants. You will never see as many bugs in your life as will appear once it gets dark. Here's where coconuts can help again. Stick the bed's legs into coconut halves filled with water. This should help keep the swarming insects occupied down below. Good news for you.

5 Starting to feel hungry? Next task: Weave a net out of coconut leaf fibers and woody vines. While you're out collecting your materials, grab some dry pieces of wood and leaves as well— you'll need them later.

6 Use your net and a sharpened stick to catch some fish. Easier said than done but, hey, what else are you going to do with your time— play video games?

7 You caught some fish. Good work! Time to make a fire. Darn, did you leave the matches at home? Get two dry pieces of wood, one flat, and one a stick. Sharpen the point of the stick. Fit it in a notch in the flat piece. Wrap some fiber around the stick so you can rotate the stick by pulling on the fibers, rather than wearing a hole in your palms. Pull back and forth, back and forth, back and forth, back and ... (you get the picture).

8 With extreme patience and perseverance—and some good luck—you will eventually get a spark. Blow on it gently. Put some dry stuff next to it to catch.

When you get a flame going, feed it tirelessly with dry wood (you did collect this earlier, didn't you?).

9 Roast fish over fire. Eat before you collapse from exhaustion.

10 Keep fire going all night. The smoke will help keep away those pesky mosquitoes that will bear down on you by the billions at dusk.

11 In the morning, stagger to your bubbly spring to quench your thirst. Then get to work drawing a giant SOS in the sand with your feet or a big stick.

12 Retire to rest in shelter during hottest part of day.

13 Repeat until rescued by pirates, film producers, or your mom.

Play in the sand and catch a wave, but not like an amateur.
You're a pro! Take these directions to the beach.

BUILD THE WORLD'S GREATEST SANDCASTLE

#36

You'll Need

sand

plastic bucket

plastic shovel or
garden trowel

**(ALL OTHER TOOLS
LISTED BELOW ARE
OPTIONAL)**

different-sized buckets,
some plain, some with
castle-type bottoms

cans (no lids)

plastic cups

putty knives or
paint scrapers

spoons

a long-handled shovel

melon-baller

first things first...

Choose the site for your château de sand. Usually, the best location is near the high-water line. If you time your building activity with the outgoing tide, you will find that the sand has the best texture, and you'll have the most time in which to work.

A flat, fine-grained sand works best for castles. Keep seaweed, shells, pebbles, and other beach bits out of your building material. They make it harder for the sand to hold its shape.

Very wet sand works best, so work quickly. If the sand starts to get dry or begins to crumble while you are still working, spritz it with water to wet it down.

Psst—this is The Secret to building great sandcastles: Never build *from the bottom up.* What you want to do is *sculpt away* from a large mound of sand, not pile sand on top of other piles, which won't be packed tightly enough to be able to support the weight on top.

1. Use your hands to scoop together a pile of sand about knee-height. Pack the pile down to compact the sand. Don't smash it down; be firm but gentle. Smooth the top so it is flat. This will be the top level of your castle.

2. Fill a pail with sand and pack it down tightly. Invert the pail at one of the four corners of your sand pile. Repeat for the other three corners.

3. Use the edge of a shovel to carve straight sides down the building and corner towers for the walls of your castle.

4. Give a decorated edge to your castle by carving out "steps" in the walls. You can cut away in some areas and not in others to give a more romantic or jaggedy effect.

5. When you are satisfied with the main structure of your castle, use your buckets or cans to form towers, turrets, and wacky rooflines. Use your putty knife or the edge of your shovel to carve doorways, windows, roof edges, or brickwork into the walls of your castle. Pencils and spoons are also good for this small work. Decorate with shiny shells, seaweed, and rocks.

Water Safety

Always **swim with a partner**—never alone.

Always body surf where there's a **lifeguard** present.

Never swim in water that is **too deep** for your swimming ability.

Avoid body surfing in **shallow water** where there is a rough ocean floor.

#37 BODY SURF

1. Figure out where the waves are breaking. (Clue: look for where all the other body surfers are standing in the water.)

2. Run into the water. Wait for the perfect wave to come your way. Warning: Never take your eyes off the incoming water!

3. A wave is coming. Turn around and begin swimming into shore. If you time it just right, the wave will overtake you just as it breaks.

4. Stop stroking, but keep kicking. Extend your arms forward, in front of your head. Streamline your body and ride that wave!

61

There's nothing nicer than sitting around the campfire on a warm summer evening. Try these favorite activities to turn a good night into a great one.

#38 ROAST THE PERFECT MARSHMALLOW

Only a true marshmallow maestro can achieve the ideal combination of silken, frothy interior and crisp, slightly caramelized outer skin.

You'll Need

marshmallows (of course)

a barbecue fork or a long, green stick from which the bark has been removed by an adult (not from a poisonous plant—check with a grown-up before using!)

a charcoal fire that has burned down to gray ash with a central hot spot of glowing red embers

1 Push a marshmallow onto the stick. Poke 1 cm (1/2 in.) of stick through the top so the marshmallow won't slip off.

2 Hold the marshmallow so it is suspended 2.5 to 7.5 cm (1 to 3 in.) above the embers.

3 Hold still for a few seconds, then begin to rotate your stick. You should see a nice, even golden crust forming as you turn. Do not hold the marshmallow in one position too long or it may fall into the fire (causing "marshmallow meltdown").

4 Once all sides have reached perfection, blow to cool the marshmallow. Then eat! Mmmm.

FIND THE BIG DIPPER

Once you know how, it's easy to spot the Big Dipper in the northern hemisphere's summer sky. To really impress other stargazers, name all seven stars that make up the Big Dipper constellation.

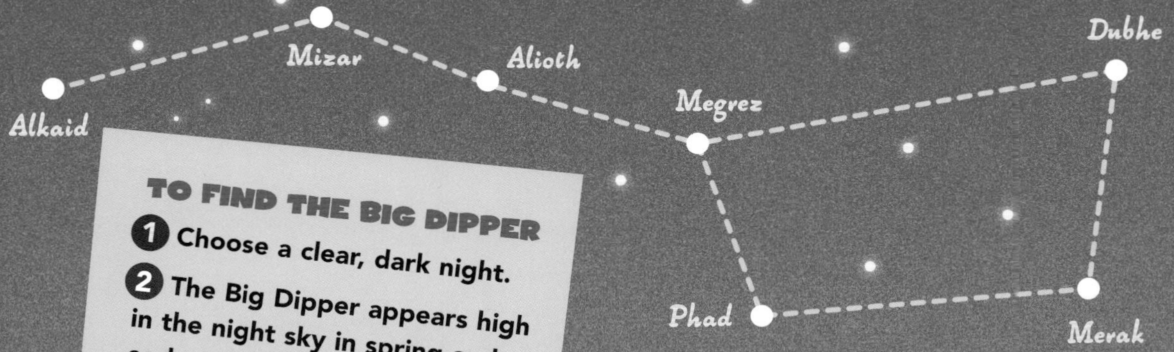

Mizar

Alioth

Dubhe

Alkaid

Megrez

Phad

Merak

TO FIND THE BIG DIPPER

1. Choose a clear, dark night.

2. The Big Dipper appears high in the night sky in spring and early summer. The best viewing time between March and June is around 10 p.m.

3. Looking toward the north, tilt your head back so that you are looking up at the sky at about a 60 degree angle. (During midsummer and autumn, the Big Dipper will be closer to the horizon, so don't look up quite so high.)

4. Find a group of stars that resemble a soup ladle. That's it! Count the seven stars.

Did you know?

The Big Dipper is part of a constellation known as Ursa Major, or the Great Bear. See the bear shape these stars form?

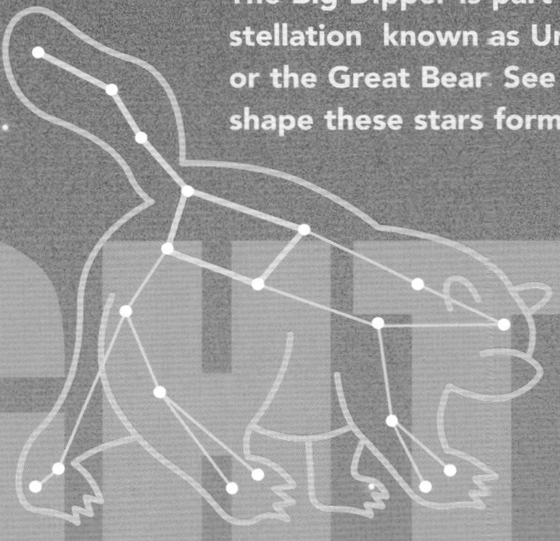

*I*t's as easy as pie to throw and catch a Frisbee®, or flying disk. Here's the recipe.

THROW A FRISBEE LIKE A PRO

Regular "Backhand" Throw

1 Set yourself up by turning sideways to your target— your throwing arm nearest to the target. Spread your feet about hip-width apart and flex your knees slightly.

2 Hold the disk with four fingers under the rim and your thumb on top.

3 Bring the arm holding the disk across your body.

4 Swing your arm forward, taking a small step forward with your front foot.

5 Release the disk with a forward wrist snap when your hand is pointing at your target. Continue your arm motion after the disk leaves your fingers. Think about rotating your shoulders and hips through to the point of release.

6 Notice if you tip the disk more to one side or the other, it will curve. With practice you'll get lots more power, and control over where your disk goes.

"Forehand" Throw (a.k.a. the Flick)

1 Stand with feet shoulder-width apart, knees slightly bent, your body turned slightly towards the target. If you're right-handed, your left shoulder is forward a bit (opposite for lefties.)

2 Hold the disc flat with two fingers underneath, thumb on top, wrist cocked back. Bring your arm back so the disk is beside your rear leg, the leading edge of the disk tilted slightly down.

3 Bring your arm forward. Snap your wrist to release the disk where your hand naturally stops (before it reaches your front leg). The force of this throw comes from your wrist snap.

CATCH THE DISK

1 Rule one: Don't be afraid of the disk. It's only a plastic toy, not a meteor hurtling towards you at the speed of light (it just seems that way). Take a deep breath and be confident.

2 The best way to catch the disk is to use both hands. When you're a real ace, you can pluck it out of the air with just one hand. All it takes is practice.

3 For a two-handed—or pancake—catch, hold both hands out in front of you (or to the side), one facing up, one facing down. Clap your hands together like a seal for a firm grip around the disk.

4 For a one-handed catch, if the disk is coming in below your waist, keep your thumb pointing up. If the disk is coming in high, keep your thumb pointing down. Use whichever position feels most natural for in-between heights. It's coming in…. Squeeze your fingers and thumb tightly together to grab the disk just before it smacks into your palm.

#41

Did you know?

In the 1940s, students at Yale University played catch using pans from a popular brand of pie. The baker's family name, Frisbie, was printed on the bottom of the plates.

KICK A SOCCER BALL TO SCORE #42

Sure you can run at the ball and swat at it with your foot. But you want your kick to get the ball into the net. Try these techniques to score a goal (almost) every time.

Practice. Practice. Practice. Sure, kicking a ball over and over again at a wall isn't as much fun as playing a game. But the game will be more fun when you have the skills you acquired from all those hours of practice.

There are lots of different **ways to kick the ball.** In all cases, make sure you are set before you kick (this means stop running!) and that your foot is lined up with your target.

INSIDE OF THE FOOT

Place your supporting foot about 10 cm (4 in.) to the side of the ball; toes point to your target. Lock the ankle of your kicking foot out at a 90 degree angle. Now bring your kicking leg back and swing—smack!—through the mid-line of the ball, making contact with the ball with the arch of your foot. Follow through, continuing your kick toward the target after the ball has left your foot. Use this kick when you're in close to the goal to score.

Kick

10 CM
4 IN.

OUTSIDE OF THE FOOT

Plant your supporting foot next to the ball, your toes pointed slightly out, at about 15–30 degrees away from your target. Swing through at the ball with your kicking foot, hitting it with the outside of your laces. Follow through and the ball should sail into the net. Use this kick to deke around a defender or to tap the ball into the net.

Kick

15-30⁰

INSTEP DRIVE

Your supporting foot lines up with the ball; toes point at the target. Bring your kicking foot as far back as you can. As you swing your leg forward, stretch out and point your toes and ankle like a ballet dancer. Kick hard, as if your foot is going to go right *through* the ball. Strike the ball with the inside of your shoelaces. Follow through toward your target. Use when you need a powerful kick.

Kick

HOW TO APPROACH A STRANGE DOG

An adorable dog strolls by while you're practicing and you need a good excuse for a break. But even cute dogs can bite. Here's how to approach one with ease.

1 Say to the owner: "Hi. Nice dog. Is he/she friendly?" Not all dogs are. Some are skittish around strangers; some are highly protective of their owners; some are just cranky. Get the ok from the owner before approaching any unfamiliar animal. (Don't ever approach a dog without an owner.)

2 If the owner says its ok, approach the dog.

3 Hold out your hand steadily beneath the dog's nose and allow the dog to sniff you. This lets the dog get used to your scent.

4 If the dog seems ok with you, you may pet it. Most dogs like to be scratched behind the ears or stroked gently along their backs.

5 If the dog's ear prick, or if it growls in an undertone, step away! This is the dog's way of saying, "Back off!"

#43

SPIN A BASKETBALL ON YOUR FINGER

Want to impress with your smooth court moves? Spinning a basketball on your finger—and making it look easy—is a valuable skill.

1 Hold the basketball up at about eye level. Your thumb should be pointing toward your face.

2 Turn your hand (to the right if the ball is in your left hand, left if in right hand) so that your pointer is now nearest your face. Balance the ball on your fingertips.

3 Quickly twist your wrist back—clockwise (left) if you're using your left hand; counter-clockwise (right) for right hand. Lift the ball up at the same time.

4 Practice step 3 (a lot) to get a fast, fluid, snapping, twisting motion that rotates the ball and gets a good, smooth spin going. This is key.

5 Point your middle or pointer finger—your choice—up under the spinning ball. Drop your thumb and other fingers. Nice!

AVOID BEE OR WASP STINGS #45

Sure you want to attract attention with your on-court moves, but of the right kind. Here's what to do to avoid the attention of stinging insects you might find on an outdoor court.

Wear light-colored clothing. Bright floral colors attract bees.

Avoid perfumed soap and shampoo. If you smell like a flower, the bee might think you are one.

Make sure your clothes and body are clean. The smell of sweat seems to aggravate bees and make them more aggressive. It doesn't do much for humans either.

Bees are most active during the warmest hours of the day. Wasps are attracted to food, so don't leave food or sweet drinks out.

Swinging or swatting at an insect may cause it to sting. Stay calm and move with gentle gestures.

If You Do Get Stung

If you or a friend do get stung, here's what to do:

• Watch for an **allergic reaction**, which may include swelling, difficulty breathing, wheezing, or dizziness. If you see any of these signs, call 9-1-1 for emergency help immediately.

• Wasps do not leave their stingers. To **remove a bee stinger**, wipe sterile gauze across the area or scrape the sting site with a credit card edge or clean fingernail. Don't squeeze the stinger or use tweezers in case you force more venom into the skin.

• Wash the sting site gently with soap and water, then apply ice to **reduce swelling**.

• To **reduce pain and itching**, dab a bee sting site with a mixture of baking soda and water. Dab a wasp sting site with vinegar. Aaahh…relief.

69

*I*t can't always be summer. But when the days turn cold, you can show you're a pro in new and different ways. Be a pro in the snow.

MAKE THE PERFECT SNOWBALL

first things first...

#46

Good snowball snow, a.k.a. "packing snow," is neither too slushy, nor too dry and powdery. Packing snow only forms in precise weather conditions: when the temperature hovers around 0° C (32° F) and when the air is not too dry. Too-dry snowballs will turn to powder as soon as you try to throw them. Too-wet snowballs turn into dangerous iceballs that no self-respecting kid would ever knowingly throw.

1 **THE SCOOP:** Kneel and place your mittened hands into the snow about shoulder-width—30 cm (1 ft.)—apart.

30 CM (1 FT.)

2 **THE SWEEP:** Sweep hands gently toward one another until you have a baseball-sized blob of snow between them—about 7.5 cm (3 in.) thick.

3 THE LIFT: Stand up with the blob of snow in your hands. Begin squeezing the snow together into a ball. Use gentle but firm pressure.

4 THE FINISH. Swivel your hands back and forth to form a smooth, even surface on your ball. It should glisten in the sun like a star.

SAFE SNOW

Never ever throw a snowball at a moving vehicle.

Never ever throw a snowball at someone's head.

Never ever ever throw an iceball.

UNSTICK YOUR TONGUE FROM A FROZEN METAL POLE

Of course you are way too smart to ever do this. But if one of your friends ever feels the urge to lick something frosty and metallic in the dead of winter, you'll know what to do. Get some warm—not hot—water. Carefully pour it over the pole and the tongue. As the pole warms up, the tongue will unstick.

#47

#48

You'll Need

packing snow
(see page 70)

waterproof mittens

carrot

stones or charcoal

1 Make a large snow-ball. Plop it into the snow on the ground in front of you.

2 Push the ball away from you, rolling it in the direction where you want your snowman to stand. As you roll, pack each layer of snow into place on the outside of the ball so it is firm and solid. Keep going until the ball is the size you want for the snowman's lower body.

3 Make a second large snowball, slightly smaller than the first. Get some friends to help you roll and lift the mid-dle ball into place on top of base ball.

4 Make the head the same way. It should be the smallest of the three balls. Lift on top of the other two.

5 When all the balls are in place, pack some snow between the layers to make sure they stick together. If your snowman seems wobbly, you can stabilize it by poking a long skinny stick straight down through the top of its head, like threading a shish kabob. Cover the hole in his head with more snow.

Be Creative!

You can use lots of different material to make faces and other features—like hair from dried-up leaves or stems from plants.

Use twigs to make arms; rocks to make buttons.
Add a scarf, or sunglasses for a "way cool" look.
Add a hat (secure it so it won't blow away)

The basic snowman body can easily be converted into a snow owl, a snow bear, or a snow dragon. Use sandcastle-building tools (see page 60) to sculpt out details.

Mix food coloring in a spray bottle to add rosy cheeks or other colorful features.

6 To make a face, use a carrot for the nose, and charcoal or stones for the eyes and mouth.

Decode Adult-Speak

Survive a Family Car Trip

At HOME

Build a House of Cards

Make a Fortune Teller

Choose a Pet

Meet and Greet Royalty

(You Never Know but Just in Case...)

Make Recycled Paper

BUILD A HOUSE OF CARDS

Always wanted to build a home of your own? Here's how.

first things first...

Ready to build? Here are the rules:

You can't use glue, tape, staples, paper clips, or any other fasteners.

You can't bend the cards to make them hang on to each other.

And don't even *think* of making notches in the cards to fit them together. That's serious cheating.

1 **Skimp on Materials.** Choose cheap, well-worn cards for best results. Really! Pro-quality cards are smooth and shiny, so they will slip off one another easily. Cheaper cards are grainier and will stay put better.

2 **Location, Location, Location.** Just like they say in the real estate biz, location is everything. Choose a space that won't get jostled by dogs and little brothers and that has a slightly textured surface, like a billiards table. A smooth surface like a glass table is a definite no-no. Avoid tablecloths, too, as they're likely to shift and cause earthquakes under your structure.

3 **Think: Zen.** Relax. Any jitters will instantly change your job from construction worker to cleanup crew. Inhale. Hold a card as lightly as a cloud between two fingers of your dominant hand. Then "float" it into place. Exhale.

4 **Build a Strong Foundation.** The key to a solidly built house is a strong foundation. In a house of cards, the foundation is a "lock box." To make it (see right):

76

Hold two cards, one in each hand, so the long edges are parallel to the table. Lean them against each other to form a slightly "off" T. Very nice.

Next, place a third card against the middle of one card to form another wonky T.

Close the box with a fourth card and T, so your lock box looks like this:

5 **Raise the Roof.** Lay two cards, face-up and side-by-side, on top of your lock box to form the roof. Add a second layer of cards, face-up on top of the first. Rotate them so they lie at a right angle to the first roof layer.

6 **One Mo' Time.** Repeat Step 4 to build a lock box on top of your roof. You now have a two-story structure. Keep building! Add wings (more T shapes) to your ground floor, then tile on more roof. Raise second, third, and fourth stories and so on until you run out of cards—or patience.

7 **Earthquake?** Play 52-card pickup, then start again!

Did you know?

Bryan Berg built a 127 story, 7.3 m (24 ft.) tall house of cards, setting a record for the world's tallest house of cards.

GET TRICKY WITH CARDS

These card tricks are easy to do, but impressive nonetheless!

THE DISAPPEARING CARD TRICK

Before you begin, prepare two sets of cards:

Set 1

Set 2

TIP

Do not repeat or answer any questions about these tricks. Just smile mysteriously and say, "Magic!" when your friend asks how you did it.

1. Conceal Set 2 beneath the table, in your lap. Say to a friend, "I can read your mind."

2. When she dares you, lay out all the cards from Set 1 face-up on the table. Say, "Choose one card in your mind. Really focus on it."

3. When your friend indicates she has one in her mind, scoop up the cards. Bring them beneath the table.

4. Say, "I am going to read your mind to find your card. I will then remove it from the pile."

5. Make it look like you are removing the card from the pile underneath the table, but while you're down there secretly swap Set 2 for Set 1.

6. Say, "Got it!" Lay the cards from Set 2 out on the table face up.

7. Say to your friend, "Is your card here?"

8. Of course, it isn't there—none of the cards are the same! But because they look so similar, your friend won't notice this fact. She will only notice that her card is missing.

9. Quickly scoop up the cards before she catches on.

1 Prepare by removing the 9 and 6 of Diamonds, and the 9 and 6 of Hearts from a complete deck.

2 Place one 9 on the top of the deck, face-down. Place the 6 of the opposite red suit (Diamonds if the 9 is a Heart, or vice versa) face-down on the bottom of the deck. Hold this deck in one hand and the other 6 and 9 in your other hand.

3 Flash the two cards in your hand quickly so your audi-ence sees the color of the suit (both are red), but doesn't register all the details. Tell them that wherever in the deck they put the two cards, you will find them instantly.

4 Have an audience member slip the cards into the deck at random.

5 Pass the complete deck behind your back. Grab it with the other hand, squeezing the top and bottom cards off the deck.

6 Bring the deck forward again. And bring the two cards around, face-down. Hold them up to the audi-ence! Ta-dah! You got the cards out of the deck in an instant! (Of course, they are not the same cards. They just look like them.)

7 Practice so you can do this trick quickly. And don't repeat for the same audi-ence or they'll catch on to the suit switcheroo.

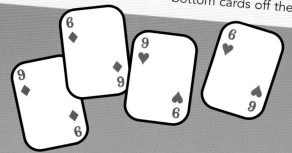

Ever wonder what your future holds?
With just a few folds of paper, you can find out.

#51

MAKE A FORTUNE TELLER

You'll Need

letter-size (8 1/2 x 11 in.)
sheet of paper

scissors

markers and other items to
decorate your fortune teller

1 Lay the paper on a table. Fold
the top right corner down
and across to form a triangle.
Line the edges up neatly.

2 Cut off the unfolded flap at
the side (in dark green).

3 Open the triangle. You
should now have a perfectly

square piece of paper. Do
you see the fold line on it?
Take one of the corners on
the fold and fold it across to
the opposite corner. Then
unfold.
Your paper
should
now be
marked
with an X.

4 Fold one corner of the
paper, so it touches the
center of the X exactly.
Repeat with
the remaining
three corners
so they all
meet in the
center.

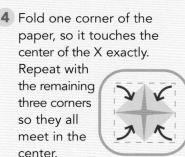

5 Flip over the paper. You
now have a smaller square
of paper with the triangular
flaps underneath.

6 Fold the corners into the
center again, one at a time,
so that the
points of
each exactly
meet in
the center.

7 See how each triangle flap
is "divided" into two smaller
triangles? There are eight
small triangle shapes all
together.
Write the
numbers 1
to 8, one on
each triangle.

8 Open up each of the four
triangle flaps and write
a fortune (or two) on the
bottom side of the flap.

9 Flip over again. See four
"squares" on this side of the
paper? Make each square a
different color or picture.

You will get a raise in your allowance.

USING YOUR FORTUNE TELLER

1 Hold the fortune teller with the numbers side face up. Fold the square in half. You will see four open square pockets, two on the front and two on the back. Hold the rectangle horizontally, so the openings are on the bottom.

2 Slip your thumbs in the two front pockets and your index fingers in the back pockets. Now bring the left and right sides of the fortune teller together, so the numbers disappear into the middle and the colored squares are on top. See how you can reveal different numbers by spreading your fingers back and forth, or side to side? You are ready to move on to Telling Fortunes.

You will travel to an exotic place.

You will master karate soon.

Great report card heading your way!

You will make a new friend.

You're a terrific pal!

TELLING FORTUNES

1 Ask a friend to choose a color (or picture). Open and close the fortune teller, in alternate directions, for every letter in the color word. If your friend chooses "red," for example, spell out r-e-d, changing the way you open the fortune teller for each letter.

2 The fortune teller will now be open. Ask your friend to choose one of the four numbers inside. Open and close the fortune teller again for the number selected. It will end up open again.

3 Have your friend choose another number. Repeat as above.

4 For the final time, when your friend chooses a number, open the numbered flap. Read him the fortune!

Anyone can make a paper airplane that nosedives off the tip of his or her fingers. But this one will fly circles around the competition.

FOLD AN ACE FLYER

You'll Need

letter-size (8 ½ x 11 in.) sheet of paper

1. Fold the paper in half lengthwise. Line the edges up carefully. Drag your fingernail along the crease to sharpen it.

2. Rotate the paper so the fold is closest to you. Fold the upper left-hand corner down to the folded edge to form a small triangle. Sharpen the crease with your fingernail.

3. Turn over the paper so the triangle is underneath it, on your right.

4. Fold the upper right-hand corner of the top layer of paper down to form a second triangle on top of the first. Sharpen the crease with your fingernail.

5. Do you see the "point" where the triangle fold begins at the top? Take it, and fold it down on a diagonal so that point meets the bottom edge. Sharpen the crease with your fingernail.

6. Fold the top layer down again on a diagonal so the top edge lines up with the bottom edge. Your top layer should now be doubled, shaped like a long, skinny triangle. Sharpen your creases.

Sharp creases and neat folds will make your plane a flying ace.

7 Turn the paper over. Repeat the last two steps (5 and 6), this time folding the diagonal down and to the right. You know what comes next...sharpen all your creases!

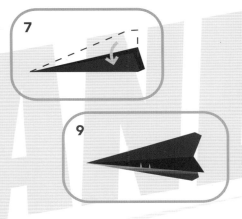

8 You have completed your basic plane shape. Grasp the plane underneath and let its wings flare out. They should be neat and flat.

9 Next, make a rudder. Slide your fingers back from the plane's "nose" about 10 cm (4 in.). Tear two rips in the bottom of the plane, each about 1.25 cm (½ in.) long. They should be about 1.25 cm (½ in.) apart. Fold the rudder up. It will help your plane fly straight.

10 To launch your plane, hold it near the rudder. Use a gentle overhand toss to send it soaring. You're a flying ace!

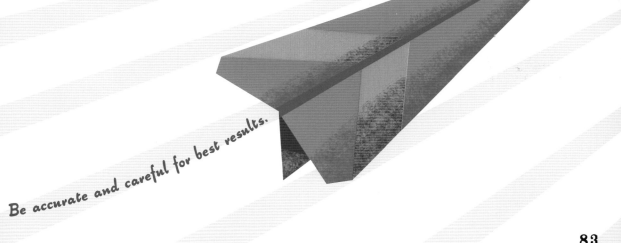

Be accurate and careful for best results.

Is your family ready to get a pet? Having a pet is one of life's greatest joys—and biggest responsibilities. Grab a pen and paper and take this quiz to see if there's a pet that is right for you. Check your answers on page 160.

CHOOSE A PET

#53

1 How much time do you have to look after a pet?

A Lots of spare time.

B A few hours a week.

C Not much spare time.

2 I want a pet that is:

A active so I can play with it.

B soft and cuddly.

C pretty to look at.

D exotic and cool.

3 My personality is:

A restless—I get bored of new things quickly.

B steady—I am reliable and fairly traditional in my tastes.

C nurturing—I love to take care of helpless things.

A New Home

Consider choosing a pet from an animal shelter. Not only will you do a good deed by providing a loving home for a needy animal, you may also receive some services—such as spaying and vaccination—free of charge.

4 In my home, we have:

A lots of space for animals to roam around.

B not much space, but enough for a small animal.

C no extra space—it's pretty crowded around here!

5 Are you squeamish?

A Very. I hate handling smelly stuff.

B So-so. I don't mind picking up after a pet but don't like cleaning out stinky cages.

C Not at all.

6 In my household, we currently have:

A dog(s).

B cat(s).

C dog(s) and cat(s).

D no pets.

7 Does anyone in your household have allergies?

A Yes.

B No.

WHERE DOES YOUR PET COME FROM?

Some animals sold as house pets are improperly captured from the wild, which endangers the environment and puts the species at risk. These can include coral reef fish, parrots, prairie dogs and exotic reptiles. Dogs are sometimes bred at "puppy mills"—little more than factories with unsanitary and inhumane conditions—before they are sold to pet stores. Such dogs risk poor health and may have been mistreated. Make sure you know exactly how the retailer obtained an animal before you buy.

Whether it's for your birthday, Halloween, or just because you feel like it, why not throw a party? To make it an event to remember, start planning well in advance.

#54 THROW A GREAT PARTY

☞ A **theme** will make your party stand out. Your theme can be whatever you like—the color red, your favorite band, or a historic era.

☞ Choose a **date** and **time**, write a **guest list**, and OK both with your family.

☞ **Make invitations** that mirror your theme. A Valentine's Day party, for example, might feature a red lip print on a white card.

☞ **Send invitations** out a few weeks in advance. Make sure to include the party particulars: **who** is throwing it (you!), **why**, **where**, and **when** (date and time). Include other details such as whether they should wear a costume. Ask guests to R.S.V.P. (**R**epondez **s**'il **v**ous **p**lait—the French words for "please reply") so you'll know how many are coming.

SUPPLY LIST
- balloons
- streamers
- loot bags
- juice, pop
- snacks

you're invited to a red & white party

☞ Plan your decorations and activities. Make a list of all the **party supplies** you will need. Include small prizes for winners of any games you plan to play.

☞ Plan your **menu**. Do you want simple munchies like chips, dips, and pop—or something fancier? Will you serve cake? What will you need to serve with?

☞ Consider how to make your **menu fit your theme**. For example, if you have a "Red and White" theme, make all the food offerings red and white. A surfing theme? Consider tropical fruit punch, fresh tropical fruits, and coconut cream pie.

Halloween Menu (Boo!)
Witch Finger Cookies
Spaghetti Brains • Spider Legs
Grape Eyeballs

☞ Plan **music** that will really get your party going. Choose songs that are popular with your crowd and any that fit your theme.

My Left Foot

You'll Need

pen and paper for each player

Have players remove the shoe and sock from their left foot. Challenge players to grasp the pen with their toes and write their name as legibly as possible. Compare!

OPEN WITH AN ICEBREAKER

Sometimes parties are slow to get going. Guests may feel shy and awkward, especially if they don't all know each other. Try playing games like these to help loosen people up and get the party started.

Mystery ID!

You'll Need

a pen, sticky notes

Make a new identity for each guest by writing the name of a famous person or character—such as James Bond or Winnie the Pooh—on a sticky note. As each guest arrives, stick an ID on his or her back. Challenge the guests to discover their Mystery ID by asking each other "yes" or "no" questions—no more than 5 questions of any single guest.

Balloon Race

You'll Need

two chairs, balloons for each player

Divide into two teams at one end of the room, chairs at the other end. On the word "Go," the first player in each team blows up a balloon and ties it. Then players run (or skip, or hop) to the chair, put the balloon on the seat, and sit on it, bouncing up and down until the balloon bursts (no hands!). Players then run back and tag the next player in line for his/her turn. The first team to pop all their balloons and return to the finish line wins.

IN FULL SWING

Your party is going full steam ahead. Keep it hopping by refilling bowls of chips and offering to refresh drinks. If the action lags, heat things up again by playing another party game.

WRAP A GIFT EXPERTLY

You'll Need

wrapping paper

transparent tape

scissors

pencil

ruler

TIPS

Work on a large, flat surface where there is plenty of light. And always make sure you remove the price tag from the gift before you wrap it.

1 Unroll enough paper that you can place the box on the extended section of paper and the paper will completely go around the box, plus a little extra. Check that there's enough paper to cover the sides.

2 Bring the loose end of the roll over the top of the box to cover it with 5 cm (2 in.) extra. Mark the paper where the extra paper overlaps. This is where you will have to cut.

3 Take the box away. Fold the paper at the pencil mark or use a ruler to draw a straight line where you need to cut. Cut the paper.

4 Put the box back in place. Eyeball the paper ends. The ends should be long enough to completely cover the box, but short enough so that they fold smoothly into flaps without crinkles and bulges. Fold the ends over the box to check and mark if you need to trim.

5 Remove the box. Cut the paper neatly at both ends where you marked.

6 Place the box in the middle of the paper, topside down.

7 Bring one long edge of the paper up around the box. Tape it in place at the center.

8 Make a neat edge at the opposite end of the paper by folding it under about 2.5 cm (1 in.).

9 Bring this edge to the center of the box to overlap the first edge taped in place. Tape the second edge to cover the first edge.

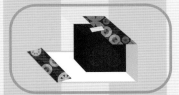

10 Turn the box so that one of the short ends faces you.

11 Fold in both sides of the paper toward the middle to form two triangular flaps, one on the top and one on the bottom.

12 Leave the flaps free for the moment and tape both sides of the paper to the box.

13 Run your fingers along the edges of the triangular flaps to make four sharp creases.

14 Press the top flap down against the box. Tape it in place.

15 Bring the lower flap up to lie flat on the box. Tape it in place. Admire your work.

16 Turn the box so the other short end faces you. Repeat steps 11–15. Your box should now be neatly wrapped in paper. Add a card and bow and you're good to go!

ALL THUMBS?

If that's how you feel, using a gift bag is the wrapping technique for you. Wrap your gift in one or two sheets of tissue paper that match or contrast with the colors of your gift bag. Place the gift in the bottom of the bag, then stuff the bag with four or more sheets of tissue paper. Or create your own gift bag. Decorate a paper bag with stamps, stickers, puff paints, glitter glue, or gel writers. And voila! Just add gift!

Who says shooting the breeze when you meet new people has to be awkward? Just use these all-yak, no-yuck conversational gambits recommended by serious yakkers to start a conversation...and keep it going.

MAKE THE CONVERSATION FLOW

Introduce yourself with a smile. Then ask the person's name. Say, "Nice to meet you, [fill in his/her name]."

Ask questions that will help you **find common ground**. For example, what's her favorite sport? Share what you like about that sport, too. This strategy works well with both kids and grown-ups.

Be positive. If your new acquaintance, says "bowling" and you loathe bowling, keep it to yourself. Ask what she likes about bowling. You may be intrigued by the answer!

Ask **open-ended questions**. Asking how she first became interested in bowling, for example, will carry your conversation longer than, "How long have you been playing?"

Stay **focused on the other person**. She will appreciate what a good listener you are!

STILL AT A LOSS FOR WHAT TO SAY?

Try one of these guaranteed conversation starters:

If you could invite any five famous people to dinner, living or dead, who would you choose and why?

You can only eat one food for the rest of your life, what would it be?

What kind of animal do you identify with most? Why?

How to Join a Conversation

The gang's yakking away, and you have something to say.

• Make sure it has something to do with **the topic** currently under discussion.

• Wait for that all-important **pause** in the conversation, when no one else is talking.

• **Take a breath** before you speak so your voice is clear and strong, and not full of pauses, ers, and ums.

How to Change the Subject

Has the conversation gotten… yawn…a little boring? Time to change the topic—gracefully.

• Make sure that everyone else is also finished with this topic. If others seem to still be riveted, just **be patient**.

• Use a segue (pronounced "seg-way") to **switch** to a topic that relates to the previous one. For example, if the conversation is about the weather but you want to talk about camping, say something like: "Talking about the weather reminds me of camping last summer. It rained so much our tent almost floated away."

Key Talking Points

• Make good **eye contact**. Look at the person who is talking—not at his buttons or the way his ears stick out.

• **Nod your head** now and then to show that you are listening and interested, and to give encouragement to the talker to continue.

• Conversations are about **taking turns** talking. Give the other person his turn, and when it's your turn, speak up.

What would you do with the money if you won the lottery?

What do you think the most interesting fortune cookie might say?

91

SET A FANCY TABLE

FOLD A FABULOUS NAPKIN

1. Fold the napkin in half to form a long rectangle.

2. Starting at one short end, fold the napkin like an accordion all the way to the opposite end.

3. Fold one short end up. Stick this end into your drinking glass. Let the napkin fan over the top of the glass.

The **FORK** sits to the left of the plate, and 2.5 cm (1 in.) up from the table edge.

Add the **SALT AND PEPPER** shakers to the table, as well as any condiments you will be using for the meal.

Using a **SALAD FORK**? Place it to the left of the first fork.

If you are serving **BREAD AND BUTTER**, you can add a small side plate to the left of the forks.

SILVERWARE SMARTS

When dining, always use the cutlery farthest from the plate FIRST. Work your way toward the middle.

If using a **TABLE-CLOTH**, lay it on the table so it hangs evenly around all edges.

NAPKIN—folded in half—can go to the left of, or beneath, the forks, or on the plate. Or, better yet, do a fancy fan fold (see left).

Add a **CENTERPIECE**, such as fresh flowers or a bowl of seasonal fruit. Keep it low so that dinner guests can see each other across the table.

GLASS goes above the knife.

Put the **KNIFE** to the right of the plate with the blade facing inward, about 2.5 cm (1 in.) from the edge of the table.

Using a **SOUP SPOON**? Place it to the right of the knife. Make sure the handle lines up with the knife, 2.5 cm (1 in.) from the edge of the table.

DINNER PLATES sit in front of each chair, about 2.5 cm (1 in.) from the table edge.

If there is a **PATTERN** on the plate, such as a rooster, make sure it stands upright, not on its head.

HAVE PERFECT TABLE MANNERS

HOW TO SIT

No, it's not as easy as parking your behind in the chair. Wait for your host to invite you to the table. She may assign you to a seat. Stand behind the chair as the other guests get assembled. When the host sits, take your seat. You'll get extra points for helping others, such as the elderly, into their seats before you take yours. After you sit, pull your chair in to the table, without dragging it over the floor with a horrible scrape. Take your napkin from the table immediately, and place it neatly on your lap. Then sit up straight, just like Mom always tells you. And keep those pesky elbows off the table, too.

HOW TO PASS ITEMS

When someone says, "Please pass the _____," reach for it only if you are the closest one to it. Take the item and place it next to your neighbor. Continue passing the item in this manner until it reaches the person who asked for it.

Refrain from helping yourself along the way, before the person who asked for it gets the chance. Wait politely until they have served themselves. Then ask for the bowl to be passed back to you.

TIP

Once you've used a utensil, don't let it touch the table again! Leave it on your plate.

Table rules seem to be a never-ending list of "thou shalt nots" and "don't you dares." Never fear. Here's how to keep them straight, and charm your hosts.

HOW TO BUTTER BREAD

When the bread basket is passed to you, you can use your hands. But take one roll or one slice of bread only. If you have a bread plate to the left of your fork, put the bread on it. When the butter is passed to you, use the serving knife to take a pat. Place it on your bread plate. Then pass the butter dish along with the serving knife to the next person. Use your fingers to tear off a bite-size piece of bread. Butter ONLY that bite-sized piece. Then eat and repeat as desired.

TIP

Follow your host's lead. Don't do anything—such as sit, start to eat, or leave the table—until he does it first, or invites you to do so.

HOW TO LEAVE THE TABLE

When everyone is finished eating, place your napkin next to your plate on the table. Wait for your host to indicate the meal is complete. Then stand up. Push your chair back in and thank your host for a delicious meal.

EAT ELEGANTLY, MY DEAR!

Use the following rules to avoid common goofs:

• Chew with your mouth closed.

• Don't talk with your mouth full.

• Don't put your fingers in your mouth or pick food out of your teeth. Excuse yourself and go to the bathroom.

• Don't bring your face down to the plate. Instead, sit up straight and bring the utensil up to your mouth.

• If anything unintended (a burp, hiccup, or food) comes out of your mouth, excuse yourself quietly. Don't make a big deal of it, and no one else will.

YOU NEVER KNOW

How to Meet and Greet Royalty

The Queen—yes, THE QUEEN—is coming for dinner! At your place! Tonight! OK, so it's the Queen of Hotzeltottle, but a queen nonetheless. Are you ready? Sure you are. Spruce up the place and follow these steps for giving your visitor the royal treatment.

#60

but just in case...

- It shouldn't need to be said, but...prepare in advance by **bathing**. Don't forget your fingernails!

- Your clothes should be neat—but **not flashy**. So skip the sequins, and press your "Sunday best."

- Ding dong! She's here. **On your feet**—no one sits when the queen is standing.

- **Bow or curtsy** if you are the queen's subject—a citizen of Hotzletottle. If not, act as if she were your very proper Great Aunt Matilda. No wriggling; stand tall.

- Welcome the queen and call her "**Your Majesty**."

- She's sticking out her hand! Good thing you cleaned those nails. **Accept the queen's hand** with a light touch. Then let go.

- **Lead the queen** into your humble abode. You must not turn your back to her, though. And don't trip, either!

- Once Her Royal Highness has settled into her chair, **don't leave the room** before she does.

- Offer the queen something to **eat and drink**. Remember, it's bad form for others to continue eating after La Queenisima has finished. When she's swallowed her last bite, so have you.

- Enjoy your **pleasant chat**. Who knew the queen loved sending prank text messages to her security staff! No one but a superior conversationalist such as yourself could have ever got her to reveal that!

- When the queen is ready to **take her leave**, she will rise from her chair. So will you. (Remember, no one sits when the queen is standing!)

- **Say goodbye**, addressing the Big Q as "Your Majesty" again. Watch her head off in her horse-drawn carriage. Sigh. Wait three seconds before calling everyone you know!

Dear Charlie,
Thanks for the snack and chat. It was so much more fun hanging with you than with all these boring old aristocrats here at the palace. I can't wait till we visit that waterpark that you told me about. I get the front of the raft, ok?

Yours truly,
The Q of H

THANKS FO

Personalize this sample below for perfect thank you notes every time!

WRITE A THANK YOU NOTE

< Today's Date >

Dear <special someone>,

Thank you so much for the wonderful <thing they gave you/did for you>. I love it because <fill in why it's special>. I will think of you every time I <wear it/use it/look at it>.

I really enjoyed <seeing you/spending time with you/talking to you> the other day. I am looking forward to <fill in upcoming activity> with you soon!

Thanks again!

<Your friend/Sincerely/With love>,

< Sign your name here >

NOTE THIS!

Make your thank you notes **specific**. Mention what it is you are thanking the person for—an item, or something he did for you—and why you appreciate it.

A **personal touch** is important. Tell something about your feelings about spending time with the person, something you remember as a highlight of your time spent together, a plan for what you would like to do together in the future, or how you will use her gift.

If you are writing to a person that you don't see often, you might also add a little note about your daily activities to **keep him up to date**.

Conclude your note with a second thank you. Then add a **suitable endearment**. "Your friend" is great for a classmate, but not so great for Great Aunt Sally.

Sign your complete name, first and last, in cursive—your handwriting—even if the letter itself is typewritten.

Yuck!

THREAD A NEEDLE #62

NO, I DON'T WANT TO GET MARRIED! I JUST WANTED YOU TO TIE THIS KNOT FOR ME!

You'll Need

a needle

thread (the same shade as your fabric, or one shade darker)

scissors

1. Cut a piece of thread that's about 60 cm (24 in.) long.

2. Dampen the thread with water and squeeze it to make the strands form a sharp point. If your thread end is uneven, trim it with scissors.

3. Hold the needle at eye level in your non-dominant hand—the hand you don't write with.

4. Hold the thread in your dominant hand, about 5 cm (2 in.) from the needle tip.

5. Guide the thread tip into the eye-hole of the needle. It may take a couple of tries. You got it!

TIE THE KNOT

Your thread's through the eye. Now you need to knot the end.

1. Pull the thread through the eye so a 10 cm (4 in.) "tail" hangs down. Leave it alone.

2. Take the other, longer end of the thread between your thumb and pointer finger. Wrap it loosely around your pointer finger three times.

3. Use the thumb on the same hand to roll and slide the thread off your pointer. It will form a tangled loop as you do this.

4. Grasp the loose loop between your pointer and thumb and pull it down toward the end of the thread to form the knot. It may take a little practice.

5. You are ready to sew!

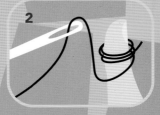

2

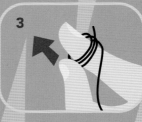

3

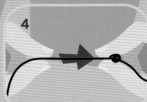

4

SEW ON A BUTTON

Here are two common types of buttons:

You'll Need

a button

needle

thread

scissors

Two-hole button

Four-hole button

Make sure your needle fits all the way through the button-hole before you begin. If not, try a smaller sized needle.

1 Thread your needle and knot the thread (see left).

2 Place your needle tip underneath the fabric, right below where the button will be.

3 Push the needle and thread up through the top of the fabric until the knot "catches."

4 Slip one hole of the button onto the needle. Pull it along the thread until it is in place.

5 Push the needle down through the second hole—all the way through the fabric to the end of the thread, so the button is held against the fabric.

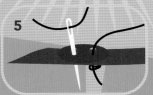

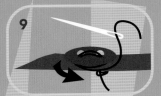

TIP

Don't attach your button too tightly. If it sits too snugly against the fabric, it will be very difficult to button up.

6 Push the needle back up through the fabric—through the first (or into the third) hole. Then back down through the second (or fourth) hole.

7 Repeat several times until the button is held firmly in place by the thread.

8 For the final stitch, bring the needle up through the fabric, but this time, don't push it through the button hole.

9 Wrap the thread around the base of the button three times to secure the threads. Stick the needle back down through the fabric, and knot.

101

Do you want to be a whiz in the kitchen? Try these simple recipes to make fabulous scrambled eggs and smoothies.

#64

SCRAMBLE IT UP

You'll Need

2 eggs per person

2 mL (1/2 tsp.) milk per egg (optional)

salt to taste (optional)

a pat of butter or margarine or 5 mL (1 tsp.) of oil

You'll Also Need

fork

microwavable bowl or mixing bowl

frying pan • spatula

1 Crack the eggs into the mixing bowl. Beat with the fork to mix the whites and the yolks.

2 Add milk to the eggs (milk makes the eggs fluffier). Add a dash of salt.

3 Now follow the steps for the Stovetop or Microwave Method of cooking.

Stovetop Method

Heat the frying pan on medium. Add butter, margarine, or oil. The pan is ready once the fat sizzles when you splash a drop of water into it. Carefully pour the egg mixture into the pan. Let it set slightly. When the eggs are partly cooked, stir them to break them up. Continue stirring until the eggs are fully cooked. Turn off the burner. Scrape the eggs off the pan onto your plates. Enjoy!

Microwave Method

Place the microwave-safe bowl with the beaten eggs in the microwave. Cook on high—about a minute—until the eggs are loosely set. Remove and stir with a fork. Return bowl to the microwave for a few more seconds if eggs aren't completely done. Serve and eat!

GET "BERRY" SMOOTH

#65

You'll Need

250 mL (1 cup) cranberry juice

½ banana

170 g (6 oz.) lemon yogurt

185 mL (¾ cup) frozen raspberries (or strawberries, blueberries, blackberries)

250 mL (1 cup) crushed ice

You'll Also Need

blender

measuring cups

1. Put all ingredients in the blender. Put the lid on.

2. Whirl on high until smooth.

3. Serve and drink up!

There are chocolate chip cookies and then there are CHOCOLATE CHIP COOKIES. Follow this recipe to whip up some that are totally out of this world.

BAKE THE BEST CHOCOLATE CHIP COOKIES

Recipe makes about two dozen cookies.

You'll Need

125 mL (1/2 cup) margarine or butter, at room temperature

65 mL (1/4 cup) white sugar

125 mL (1/2 cup) brown sugar, packed

5 mL (1 tsp.) vanilla extract • 1 egg

250 mL (1 cup) flour

2.5 mL (1/2 tsp.) baking soda

2.5 mL (1/2 tsp.) salt

250 mL (1 cup) chocolate chips

You'll Also Need

large mixing bowl • measuring cups

measuring spoons • mixing spoon

electric mixer (optional)

nonstick cookie sheets

spatula • cooling rack • oven mitts

1. Preheat oven to 190°C (375°F).
2. In a large bowl, blend the butter or margarine with the brown and white sugars thoroughly until the mixture is light and fluffy, about one minute.
3. Add the vanilla extract and the egg. Beat the mixture thoroughly, for about 30 seconds with an electric mixer.
4. Stir in the flour, baking soda, and salt. Add the chocolate chips. Make sure the mixture is well blended.
5. Drop the mixture by the teaspoonful onto an ungreased cookie sheet. Place cookies about 5 cm (2 in.) apart.
6. Bake for 8 to 10 minutes, until cookies are golden. Watch so they don't burn!
7. Remove the cookie tray carefully from the oven, using oven mitts. Have a grown-up help you with this step. Leave cookies on the tray for a few minutes.
8. Using a spatula, remove the cookies from the tray and move them to a cooling rack. When cool enough to eat, pour yourself a tall glass of milk, and dig in!

SAFETY FOR BUDDING CHEFS

Cooking is fun, but any time you work with heat or sharp implements, accidents can happen. Use this guide to stay safe in the kitchen!

Always pass knives or scissors to another person by the handle.

When cooking on the stove, lift off pot lids at an angle to steer any steam away from your face.

Always check that stove burners and ovens are turned off when you are finished using them.

Never put metal containers in the microwave. The microwave can zap them—zzzt-zzzt-zzzt!

Never leave pots unattended on the stove.

Clean up spills immediately to prevent slips.

Use potholders when handling hot objects.

Don't let fabrics or long hair swing freely near stoves or toasters. They can catch fire.

Keep towels, potholders, and any paper goods away from a hot stove!

Turn pot and pan handles toward the wall. Then you'll be less likely to bump into them and spill hot soup or food on yourself.

Got a secret you want to keep hush-hush but still share with your best friend? Or want to talk in a language no one else can understand? Try speaking in one of these codes.

SPEAK IN CODE

PIG LATIN

Start with a word—any word—such as "cheese." Take the ch- sound off the beginning of the word. Now you've got "eese." Then tack the ch-sound on the end of the word, and add an "ay." Now you've got "eese-chay." Congratulations! You've just spoken your first word in Pig Latin. "Eese-chay" is Pig Latin for cheese. Do the same thing to every word in your sentences. If a word starts with a vowel, just leave it and add "ay" to the end. For example, the word "end" is pronounced "end-ay." Try it, saying a simple sentence such as, "Pig Latin is easy." Check your answer on page 160. Asn't-way at-thay imple-say?

UBBI-DUBBI

This secret language is a little bit tougher for people to decipher, but it's simple to speak. Just add an "ub" sound in front of every main vowel in a word. For example, the word "cheese" is pronounced "chubeese" in Ubbi-Dubbi.

SPEAKING IN RARE TONGUES

Do lots of kids in your 'hood already know Pig Latin and Ubbi-Dubbi? If so, try speaking in one of these rare tongues or codes. Or make up one of your own!

Backwardspeak

To speak this code language, take the last sound in each word and transfer it to the front of the word. For example, "cheese" becomes "zuh-chee."

Backwardspeak 2

This language is hard to speak without writing it down first. You pronounce each word as if you are reading it from right to left. For example, "cheese" becomes "eseech."

I Spy Language

Replace every vowel with a long "i" sound. For example, "cheese" becomes "Chise."

Killer Bs

Add a "b" after every vowel. Then repeat the vowel. So "cheese" becomes "chebeebesebe."

DECODE A MESSAGE

FOR YOUR EYES ONLY

Can you decipher this Ubbi-Dubbi message? Check your answer on page 160.

Whuby ubam Ubi spubendubing muby vubalubuubable tubime duboubing tาubis crubazuby subecrubet lubangubuage thubing?

Ever notice that what adults say and what they mean frequently seem to be two different things? Maybe that's why you sometimes get sent to your room, without having a clue why. Here's the translation manual.

DECODE ADULT-SPEAK #68

You Hear: Is that outfit the best you have?

They Mean: Change out of that horrible attire ASAP!

You Hear: Do you have any homework?

They Mean: Do your homework now!

WOULD YOU LIKE TO CLEAR THE TABLE NOW?

NO THANKS! I'D RATHER WATCH TV.

CLEAN THE TABLE RIGHT NOW!!!

You Hear: Did you hear me?

They Mean: Do whatever I just asked you to do right now.

You Hear: How do I look in this outfit?

They Mean: Tell me I look great!

You Hear: What did you do in school today?

They Mean: Tell me every single thing you did, even when you went to the bathroom.

You Hear: Make sure to brush your teeth before bed.

They Mean: Brush each tooth with toothbrush and toothpaste. And don't skip the floss. And clean up after yourself when you are through. And wash your face with soap and warm water. Do the ears, too. Dry your hands—on a towel.

Not THAT towel— that's for guests. The other one. And put it back folded just like it was before. And turn off the water so it doesn't drip the way you always leave it. And while you're at it, put out a new roll of toilet paper, puh-lease!

You Hear: How long have you been playing that video game?

They Mean: Turn it off, pronto!

You Hear: I love you!

They Mean: I love you!

CLEAN UP

Ever feel the urge to tidy up your room? Didn't think so. So here's a handy tip: If you get into the habit of making your bed daily, your room will seem neater with hardly any effort.

MAKE YOUR BED

STEP 1: PUTTING ON THE SHEETS

1 Lay the bottom, fitted sheet on top of the mattress.

2 Pull the sheet elastic over the mattress corner closest to you. Then pull the sheet elastic over the corner to the left or right. Go to the other end of the bed and pull the sheet elastic over the third corner.

3 Now comes the tricky part—the last corner. You may have to lift up the mattress corner to get the fitted sheet over it. Use your muscles!

4 Smooth the sheet by pulling it down around the mattress and tucking it under the mattress around all sides.

5 Now unfold the top sheet. Flip it so the pattern is on the underside if there's a design on the sheets.

6 Stand at the bottom of the bed holding the end of the sheet in both hands. Raise and lower your arms so the sheet flies up then falls down evenly, so there is about the same amount of overhang on both sides of the bed.

7 Smooth the top sheet. If you like a snug bed, tuck all the loose edges of the sheet under the mattress.

8 Replace your pillowcases when you change your sheets.

STEP 2: THE BLANKET OR COMFORTER

1 Stand at the bottom of the bed and hold the end of the blanket or comforter in your hands. Raise and lower your arms to flare the blankie up in the air. Let it fall down evenly on the bed.

2 The blanket should hang the same amount over both sides of the bed. The top edge of it should lie about 20 cm (8 in.) below the end of the top sheet. Fold the top sheet down over the blanket edge to finish. Now if there's a pattern on the sheet, you'll see it facing the right way.

Don't want to go to the trouble of making your bed every day? Practice the art of lying completely still as you sleep. Think: I am Dracula. Then, when you get up in the morning, all you'll have to do is flip the blanket back into place.

#70 HAMMER A NAIL

Has your clean room motivated you to make some room improvements? Check with your parents first, of course, but here's how to hammer in that picture hook with a little know-how.

1 Choose the right tool. A medium weight hammer is best for most jobs. You will need the claw end for certain jobs, like removing nails.

2 Hold the hammer near the end of the handle, not the head, to swing it. This will give you more hitting power.

3 Choose the right nail for the job. It should be long enough to grasp with your fingers. It should also be strong enough and long enough to hold whatever you are hanging on it (like a picture), or connecting together (like two pieces of wood).

4 Hold the nail below the head with the fingers of one hand. Place it where you want it. Tap it gently with the hammer to set it in place.

5 When the nail is set and sticks in place when you let go, grasp the hammer firmly at the end and hit the nail straight on. A few smacks should knock it into place.

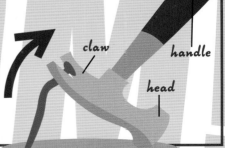

claw

handle

head

It's green, it's wet, it's home. It's Planet Earth, and it's the only one we've got. So use these energy saving tips to keep it healthy for a long, long time.

BE GREEN

#71

Get Sun Smart

Is the summer sun beating in and turning your bedroom into a sauna? Keep your cool by drawing curtains or blinds during the hottest part of the day. In the winter, let the sun shine in for some extra (and free!) warmth and cheer.

Keep Cool

Don't turn your home into an icebox in the summer. Turn your thermostat up a few degrees to reduce the amount of energy you use to power up the air conditioning (AC). Use a fan whenever possible. If your home has a ceiling fan and AC, turn on the fan and turn the AC down—the moving air will keep your house cooler than just AC alone. This smart combo lets you keep your cool but takes far less energy to run.

Turn It Down

Do you really need your home to be baking hot in the winter? Turn the thermostat down a notch, and stay cozy by throwing on a warm sweater. Each one-degree change means a savings of up to 5 percent on your home's heating costs!

TIP

Is there a light that everyone forgets to turn off, like the one in the bathroom? Make a sticker or a sign that says "Turn me off—please!" and hang it next to the switch.

Turn me off PLEASE!

Plant Trees

If you've got the space, your family could plant trees in the yard around your home. They will help keep your home cooler during the summer, and keep the air fresher year-round. You can also suggest a tree-planting program at your school. How about a school challenge: Which class can raise the most money to plant new trees on your school's grounds?

En-light-en Yourself

Discuss with your family using some low-energy lightbulbs. They last much longer than traditional bulbs and use only a fraction of the energy. They also last for years, meaning you'll save yourself the energy it takes to change them!

Use Your Own Steam

Use human power whenever you can. Walk, bike, or rollerblade to school instead of getting your parents to drive you. Hang laundry on a clothesline instead of using the clothes dryer. Use a push mower instead of a gas-guzzler to cut your grass. Human power is good for the planet's health, and for your own health too!

FIGHT THE LIGHT!

If every kid followed this one rule alone, we'd save tons and tons of energy: Turn off lights and electronic equipment—TVs, stereos, and computers—when you finish using them. At school, why not suggest that your class appoint an energy monitor each week to check that lights and computers are turned off during recess, lunch, and at the end of every day.

Turn yesterday's news into today's newsflash by writing up the latest goings-on on sheets of paper you recycle yourself.

MAKE RECYCLED PAPER

You'll Need

old clean **newspaper** or other **waste paper**

water

dishpan

electric blender

20 cm x 20 cm (8 in. x 8 in.) piece of window screen

old towel

30 cm x 30 cm (12 in. x 12 in.) piece of old bedsheet

dry sponge

1. Rip up your paper scrap into small pieces. Place them in a dishpan filled with water. Soak overnight.

2. The next day, place two or three handfuls of the soggy paper mixture in the blender (with your parents' permission). Fill the blender about half full with water. Turn on the blender in short bursts to break up the paper into mush.

3. Lay the window screen in your dishpan. Fill the pan with about 7.5 cm (3 in.) of water. Pour the pulp from the blender over the screen in the dishpan.

4. Gently slide the screen back and forth through the mixture to break up any clumps. Then lift the screen straight up. The pulp should be spread evenly on top of the screen.

5. Put the screen on a towel to drain.

6. Lay the piece of sheet on top of the pulp on the screen.

TIP
You can add color to your paper by adding two or three drops of food coloring to your pulpy mixture in the blender (at step 2).

7 Press down firmly on the sheet with the dry sponge to squeeze out all the excess water from the paper pulp.

8 Lift up the screen and turn it over. The paper should release onto the sheet. Lay it on a flat surface to dry overnight.

9 When the paper is dry, carefully peel it away from the cloth.

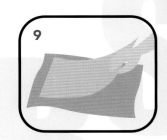

TIP

You can dry the paper faster and make it smoother by placing the paper between two sheets of fabric and pressing it with a warm iron.

NEWSFLASH

FROM YOURS TRULY

Now you can create your own newspaper with all the news of your world. Don't forget the flashy headlines.

Childs Loads Dishwasher—Unasked!

School Fun Run a Runaway Success

Spooky Sleepover Party Planned for Friday the 13th at Hill Street House of Horrors

Put on your most pleasant "dial tone" when you answer the phone by following these dos and don'ts of phone etiquette.

HONE YOUR "DIAL TONE"

Answering a Wrong Number

For a wrong number, say: "I'm sorry, you've dialed the wrong number." It's acceptable for the caller to check the number dialed by saying, "Is this 555-2222?" But it's not acceptable for the caller to ask more. Do not give out any personal information to an unknown caller!

Taking a Message

Once you say to a caller, "So-and-so isn't here right now, may I take a message?" Guess what? You have to take the message! So write down the caller's full name and phone number and read it back to them to make sure you got it right. Then put the neatly written message in a spot where your mom, dad, or big sis will find it and return the call.

Ending a Call

You've been chatting with your friend, but now you really need to finish your homework. Plus your mom is signaling that she needs the phone. How do you end your call without offending your friend? Try the truth: Say that you have to go and your mom needs the phone. If she keeps on talking, jump in with, "I'm sorry, I hate to cut you off, but...." This should do the trick.

HOME ALONE?

If you answer the phone when your parents are out, don't say, "No one else is here right now." Say, "My parents can't come to the phone right now. May I take a message?" It's not safe to let a caller know you are at home alone.

116

Handling a Nuisance Call

The best way to handle a nuisance call is to hang up. Don't speak to the caller. If the caller says something rude or scary, tell an adult. If no adults are home, don't answer the phone again. If the phone keeps ringing, pick up the receiver, hang it up again immediately, then leave it off the hook.

DECODE TEXT MESSAGES

Check out these text messages. Can you match them to their meanings? By the time you've solved them all, you'll be a text message pro. Check your answers on page 160.

BTW   CUL8R   GR8   HHIS   LOL   L8R G8R

CU 2MORO   ROFL   THX or TX   WERV U BIN

YKWYCD   YYSSW   B4N   BF   DTS

GMTA   HF   HRU   IDK   JJA   MoS

NW   PU   RME   SIG2R   SOMY   SUP

Thanks	No way!	Don't think so
Mother over shoulder	Sorry, I got to run	See you later, alligator!
How are you?	Great!	Sick of me yet?
Great minds think alike	Rolling my eyes	By the way
I don't know	Laugh out loud	Where have you been?
Yeah, yeah, sure, sure, whatever	That stinks!	Call you later
You know what you could do	See you tomorrow	Best friend
Have fun	Hanging my head in shame	Bye for now
What's up?	Rolling on the floor laughing	Just joking around

#74

You're forced to sit still for hours. Your captors include one who ignores you, one who blares opera, and one who insists on poking you with a small action figure. You are on a—Arrghhh!—family car trip! Here are some distractions to keep you from cracking up.

#75 SURVIVE A FAMILY CAR TRIP

You'll Need
colored pencils
paper

AUTO BINGO

1 First, create your bingo boards as shown.

2 In each box except the center box, write or draw something that you're likely to spot on your trip—a seagull, stop sign, tollbooth, bridge, red barn, truck, and the like. Make each board somewhat different. Then as you ride along, look for the items on your bingo board. Mark off each box as you spot the item in it. The first player to mark off all the boxes on his or her board wins.

AVOID GETTING CARSICK

Keep your eyes on the road ahead. Sitting in the middle back seat or the front passenger seat—if you're big enough—will give a better view of the road. Don't read or look at anything that may move inside the car.

LICENSE DECODER

Vanity plates are everywhere. People buy these personalized licenses to send a message about themselves. Can you decipher these wacky license plates and match each one to the kind of person it belongs to? (Check your answers on page 160.) Can you make up your own, too?

SPOT THAT LICENSE PLATE

How many license plates from each different state, province, and territory can you spot on your trip? Make a list to record each different one you see. Pool your results with other passengers for best results.

THE COW GAME

One team takes the left side of the road; the other the right. Keep count of every time you see a cow on your side. Sound easy? Every time you pass a cemetery, you lose all your points. At the end of the drive, the team with the most points gets to choose a treat.

NAME THAT TV SHOW

In this game, having watched too much TV is an advantage. The first player hums a theme song from a television program. The other players then try to name the TV show it comes from. A point goes to whoever guesses the correct show first. If no one guesses correctly, the hummer gets a point. The player who scores the point gets to hum the next theme song. The game ends when you run out of songs, or one player scores 10. Variation: Successful guessers can add an extra point to their score if they can sing all of the words correctly, too.

VET DR

IISK8R

QTPI

W8LIFTR

10SNE1

8 2 MUCH

2BZ

HIHO

Did they finally let you out of the car? Of course, now you're trapped at a roadside motel and it's pouring rain outside! Thank goodness for your survival kit (this book).

AMUSE YOURSELF ON A RAINY DAY

THUMB WRESTLING

You'll Need

two players

1 Both players extend their right hands (or left hands). Bend your fingers and hook them together to make a double "c" shape with your hands. Both players' thumbs should be able to lie flat on the tops of your fists and wiggle freely in the air. Place your hands and your lower arms down on a table.

2 Cross your thumb over the other player's, then return it to its original position a few times. You can chant while you are doing this (see below). As soon as you finish the chant, start your battle! Each player will try to trap the other player's thumb under his or her own. You cannot unclasp your hand from your opponent's, use any other finger to help out, or lift your arm or hand from the tabletop. If you catch your opponent's thumb, you must hold it down for a count of three before you may be declared the winner.

1, 2, 3, 4, WE WILL HAVE A THUMB WAR; 5, 6, 7, 8, TRY TO KEEP YOUR THUMB STRAIGHT.

TABLE SHUFFLEBOARD

You'll Need

a penny • 2 pens or pencils

1. Hang the edge of the penny off your side of the table.

2. Align one pen about 2.5 cm (1 in.) from the table edge to mark where your end zone is. Have your opponent do the same.

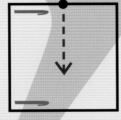

3. You have three turns to get your penny as close to your opponent's edge of the table without sliding off. Use your index finger to nudge the penny toward the "goal."

4. Score a point for getting your penny into the endzone; three points for hanging over the table edge without falling.

TABLE FOOTBALL

He shoots, he scores! Fold up a paper napkin into a small triangle—your table football. Have your opponent join his thumbs and hold up his forefingers to make two goal posts across a table. From your side of the table, flick your football toward the goalposts. Did you get it through? Score! Now it's your opponent's turn.

TWIDDLE YOUR THUMBS

Keep your thumbs limber for a big wrestling match! Clasp your hands together, interlacing the fingers. Hold your palms apart, your two thumbs parallel to one another. Swivel your thumbs around each other—faster and faster! Then in reverse.

BOX THE DOTS

You'll Need

paper

two pencils or pens

1. Draw 10 rows of 10 evenly spaced dots.

2. The hungriest player goes first.

3. Players take turns drawing a horizontal or vertical line connecting any two dots. Diagonal lines are not allowed.

4. Players look for three lines that form three sides of a box. When they can draw a line between the remaining two dots to close the box, they write their initials in it.

5. The object of the game is to make the most boxes.

6. Every time players close a box, they get another turn. Once they run out of boxes to close, their opponent takes a turn. Players may not skip any turns.

Make a Wish
ANYWHERE
Take Fabulous Photos
Start Your Own Business
Beat a Bad Mood

How to Prepare for a Space Mission

Be Street Smart

(You Never Know but Just in Case...)

and

EVERYWHERE

Make a Square Bubble

Wet Your Whistle

Who wouldn't want some extra cash in the bank or to go toward that cool new gadget you've been eyeing at the electronics store? Here are some great ideas so you can work for yourself, doing something you love.

#77 START YOUR OWN BUSINESS

Step 1 Decide what you want to do.

Your business should be one that you enjoy, are good at, and that customers will want to pay you to do. For example, if you like to make other kids laugh, a clown/party entertaining business might be right up your alley. Prefer physical work? Consider lawn work, shoveling snow, and/or raking leaves.

TIP

Do an actual survey of potential customers to see if they might be interested in hiring you. Find out how much they would be willing to pay too!

Step 2 Draw up a business plan.

Once you've decided on the type of business, get serious by putting your plan in writing. Your plan should include details such as what supplies you need, their cost, who your potential customers are, your potential earnings, and your time commitment. Don't rush into anything!

The money used to start a business is called "**capital**." You invest capital in a business with the idea that your money will grow more than it would if you invested it somewhere else, such as a savings account. Someone—say, a family member—might invest in your great idea with a loan that you'll pay back once your business is thriving.

type (word process)
schoolwork for other kids

shovel snow

teach computers to your
parents or grandparents

take pet
pictures

babysit   wrap gifts

make greeting cards   wash cars

do garden care—
weeding and watering

pet sit

make jewelry   walk dogs

rake leaves

LAUNCHING YOUR BUSINESS

You've done all your prep work. Now you're ready to start making money. Follow these steps for a successful launch of your new business.

Step 3   Gather your resources.

What supplies do you already have? What do you still need? How much money will you need to buy the other supplies you need? Last but not least, do you have all the skills you will need to successfully deliver what you promise? For example, if you'd like to be the best babysitter on the block, do you need to first improve your skills by taking a course? If so, how much will the course cost, and how long will it take until you are certified or ready to go to the next step?

Start small. Test out your business on a few clients, preferably family or friends. If you run into problems, they will be supportive as you fine-tune your skills.

Your First Customer.
You're in business! Hooray! Do exactly as promised. Be polite, on time, accurate, business-like, and responsible.

Market yourself.
You've got to let potential customers know about your business, right? Word of mouth is a great way to advertise. Tell everyone you know about your new business. Encourage friends and family to spread the word.

125

*N*ow that your business is underway,
keep up the good work by analysing your success.

JUDGE HOW YOU'RE DOING

First, are you enjoying the business you launched? Or is it taking too much time away from your schoolwork or friends? Next, ask yourself: Are you doing what you expected you'd be doing? Do you have the number of customers you estimated you'd have? Are you earning what you thought you would? What about expenses: Did launching the business cost more than expected? Are the supplies you need on a regular basis more costly? To make sure you're not paying out more than you're earning, take a close look at your profits and losses (see right).

WHAT TO WATCH OUT FOR

If earring supplies cost $5, and you're selling the finished product for only $4, you are *losing money on every item you sell!* If your costs for each job or item sold are higher than your income you will either have to charge more for your product or reduce your costs.

BREAKING EVEN

Once you know how much money you are making, you can figure out when you'll "break even" (the point at which your business can pay you back for your capital investment). Let's say you invested $35 in supplies for your leaf-clearing job. Since you earn $9.50 every time you rake a lawn, you will earn enough money to pay yourself that $35 back after you have raked 4 lawns ($9.50 x 4 = $38.00).

THROW IN THE TOWEL?

If your business isn't working out the way you'd like, don't be too discouraged. Many very successful businesses were created by people who failed their first few times. Whether you stay in business or throw in the towel, you'll have gained skills and experience.

SAFETY FIRST

Never get so hungry for success that you forget about your safety. Discuss your business ideas with your parents, and make sure that your customers are known neighbors, family, and friends. When you're off to a job, keep your parents in the loop about where you're going and how long you expect to be gone.

THE PRO'S GUIDE TO PROFIT AND LOSS

• **Make two columns** on a sheet of lined paper. Label the lefthand column "Income," and the right-hand column "Expenses."

• Under **Income**, write down how much money you took home from each job you performed. Total the earnings, and put this number on the bottom line.

• Under **Expenses**, list absolutely everything you spent money on: the job supplies, advertising (creating flyers, etc.), gas money paid to your mom for driving you to that job. Total your expenses on the bottom line.

• **Compare** your expenses to your income. If your income is larger, congratulations, you are making money! If your expenses are higher, you need to look a little closer.

• Subtotal all your **start-up expenses**— what you purchased with your "capital invest-ment" to get the business running. Let's say you spent $15 for a rake, $8 on leaf bags, and $12 to create flyers, for $35 total.

• You want your business to make enough money to pay back your capital investment AND generate cash for the future, right? To see if you are on the right track, subtract all of your one-time capital (start-up) expenses from the total expenses. The remaining amount is what you're spending to operate your business (**operating expenses**).

• **Compare** your operating expense total to your income total. Your income total should be higher than your expense total. If so, you are making money! If your day-to-day expenses are **more** than your income, find out why. Are you charging too little for your services? Or perhaps you didn't consider the on-going costs of supplies. Make adjust-ments to your practices before you continue.

INCOME

(Oct 3) $15.00
(Oct 10) $10.00
(Oct 11) $15.00
(Oct 12) $5.00
(Oct 17) $20.00
(Oct 24) $5.00

TOTAL: $70.00

EXPENSES

(how-to books) $7.50
(photocopies) $2.50
(bus tickets) $10.00

TOTAL: $20.00

Success!

BE THE BEST BABYSITTER ON THE BLOCK

Do you have what it takes to be a family's favorite sitter? Most parents look for babysitters that have certain basic characteristics. These include:

dependability
Reliability is first and foremost. You are responsible for their child's health and safety.

love for little kids
The best babysitters enjoy being around younger children.

maturity
Can you keep a cool head in an emergency?

good manners
This means you don't snoop around, spend hours on the phone, or eat them out of house and home.

safety smarts
If you know what to do in case of a fire, as well as basic first aid and lifesaving techniques, you and your clients will feel more confident about how you'd cope in an emergency situation.

self-confidence
If you're sure of yourself, your charges will be sure too.

knowledge
Expert babysitters know the basics for feeding, dressing, diapering, bathing, and playing with children of different ages.

THE BUSINESS OF BABYSITTING

Babysitting is a job. As with any business arrangement, you should set out the financial details up front. Find out what the going rate is for babysitters in your neighborhood. Your rate should be in the same range—more for looking after more kids or if you have lots of experience, less if you are new at the job. Discuss the rate with the client—before you accept the job.

Babysitter's Checklist

EMERGENCY NUMBERS

You need to know:

- Fire department*
- Police department*
- Ambulance *
- Poison control hotline
- Veterinary emergency hotline (if there are pets in the house)
- Phone numbers for neighbors and other family members (in case the parents aren't reachable)
- Address and phone number where you are so you can give it to a 9-1-1 operator in an emergency

* 9-1-1 may take care of all three (see page 132).

PARENTS' INFORMATION

You need to know:

- Parents' cellphone and/or pager number
- Address and phone number of where the parents are going
- When the parents expect to get to their destination and when they expect to leave
- What time they think they'll be returning home
- Whether they are expecting any phone calls or visitors
- How/if they would like you to answer the door and phone if anyone calls.

INFORMATION ABOUT THE CHILD

You need to know:

- Meals: What and when should the child(ren) eat? Any food allergies or restrictions?
- Medication: Never give any medication unless the parents have given you instructions. If a child has an epi-pen (for severe allergic reactions) the parent should train you in how to use it.
- Bedtime: When? Is there a special bedtime routine?
- Bathtime: Never, ever leave a child alone in a bathtub!

INFORMATION ABOUT THE HOME

You need to know:

- Where locks, alarms, and extra keys are, and how they work
- Emergency supplies: flashlights, first aid, and cleaning products
- Appliances: Make sure you know how to work the can opener, stove, oven, microwave, high chair, heat or air conditioning
- Pets: Will pets need to be fed or given water—when, what, and how much?
- Many communities offer courses in babysitting and first aid. Try to do one of these before your first job.

*S*kinned your knee? Sliced your finger? Follow these basic how-tos to become a pro at taking care of minor injuries.

CLEAN A WOUND

You'll Need

soap and running water

sterile swabs or tissues

bandages

#79

1. Clean the wound with soap and water using the sterile swabs and tissues.

2. Pat the wound dry. If it's still bleeding, compress the wound gently to encourage clotting and stop the bleeding.

3. Cover the wound with an adhesive bandage (see instructions at right) and tell a responsible adult about the injury. Depending on the situation, they may decide your injury needs further attention. Puncture wounds, very deep wounds, and injuries to your face may require professional attention.

APPLY A BANDAGE **#80**

1. Clean and dry the wound as described at left.

2. Choose the right-sized bandage to cover the area effectively.

3. Open the wrapper and peel off one piece of the paper that covers the self-adhesive strips. Do not touch the central pad—you want it to stay sterile.

4. Apply the bandage so that it follows the natural curve of your body. If the cut is on a finger or toe, place the strip so it will be able to wrap around the digit.

5. Fasten the first sticky side of the bandage onto your skin so that the pad lies over the wound. Then remove the second strip of paper, and pull the bandage into place. Press with your fingertips to secure.

BASIC

REMOVE A BANDAGE—THREE WAYS

Getting the bandage into place is a walk in the park compared to removing it.
Suffer not! Here are three great ways to remove a bandage without tears.

Method A:
The Quick Method

Grab one end of the bandage. Close your eyes and take a deep breath. Count to three. On three, yank the bandage off as fast as you can. Immediately apply a chunk of ice or a cold compress to the area.

Method B:
The S–L–O–W Method

Gently work at one corner of the bandage. Lift it; tug it a little. Ignore. Repeat a few moments later. Keep tugging and wiggling slowly until the bandage comes off, or you give up and resort to Method A.

Method C:
The Prizewinner's Method

Soak a cotton ball in baby oil or olive oil. Rub the ball over the top of the bandage—back and forth over the sticky sections. The oil will dissolve the adhesive and…. Hooray! The bandage will slip off.

RST AID

OUCH!

KNOW WHEN TO CALL 9-1-1

#82

The fastest way to get emergency help is by dialing 9-1-1 on your phone. An emergency operator—called a dispatcher—will answer your call. The dispatcher must know exactly where you are, and exactly what is wrong. Operators are connected to police, firefighters, and ambulance crews. Depending on what you say, they will send one or more types of emergency workers.

When to Call

You should call 9-1-1 ONLY if a person is badly hurt or in danger RIGHT NOW. Reasons for calling include:

- witnessing a car accident

- a crime in progress

- someone hurting someone else

- when someone suddenly seems very ill, is having a hard time breathing, or turns blue

- if someone collapses or passes out

- if there is a fire

- if someone is having a severe allergic reaction

#83 REMOVE A SPLINTER

You'll Need

soap and warm water

disinfectant such as rubbing (isopropyl) alcohol

tweezers

cotton ball

needle

bandage

1. Clean the area with soap and water or a disinfectant spray.

2. Clean and disinfect your tweezers.

3. Grasp the tip of the splinter with the tweezers. Pull it slowly along the track of entry. Lightly squeeze the skin in the same direction, pushing the splinter toward the surface of the wound.

4. If the splinter breaks or is not sticking out of the wound, you may need to use a needle. Sterilize the needle, then slip it into the hole made by the splinter and try to get a hold of the splinter tip. See if you can wriggle the splinter into a better position or pull it out with the needle.

5. Once you remove the splinter, squeeze the wound a little to encourage bleeding. This will help clean out the wound.

6. Apply an adhesive bandage.

If you do call 9-1-1

Stay calm. Take a few deep breaths if you need to.

Speak clearly. The dispatcher needs to understand you to help.

Be prepared to answer questions from the dispatcher: What is the emergency? What happened? Where are you? Where do you live? Who needs help? Who is with you? Are you safe where you are?

Follow the dispatcher's directions. Don't hang up until the dispatcher has told you that it is OK.

Do Not Call 9-1-1

• when you are still in immediate danger. If you can, get to safety before you make a call.

• if your pet is in trouble. Call a veterinary emergency service.

• on a dare.

• if you have a minor injury.

Never, ever call 9-1-1 as a joke or just to see what might happen. When the dispatcher has to take the time to talk to people who don't have a real emergency, other people who call and do need help right away might have to wait.

TAKE FABULOUS PHOTOS

#84

A picture's worth a thousand words, right? But only if it's a *good* picture. Follow this snap-happy guide to turn your pics into prizewinners, every time.

Don't point the camera into the sun. Stand with **your back to the sun**, so your subject's face will be lit up rather than cast in shadow.

Some cameras have a special "**red eye** double flash." If yours doesn't, ask your subjects to look above your head when you snap the shot.

A **flash** can only work about 2.5 to 3 m (8 to 10 ft.) ahead. So don't bother trying to snap the starry sky. Your flash won't be able to light it up at such a long distance.

Don't stand **too close** to your subject when using your flash either or you'll just get a whiteout.

Before you click, look at **what is behind** and near your subject. Looks like this poor kid is having a pretty bad hair day!

Poor Tammy lost her head! Make sure your subject is **completely in the frame**.

Zoom in close to give your subject more impact. Teeny figures don't make for interesting shots.

For added interest, follow the **"rule of thirds."** Mentally divide your picture into nine equal sections, like a tic-tac-toe grid. Line up your subject one-third of the way over from the left. Emphasize the background in the remaining two-thirds. Then line up your horizon one-third of the way from the top or bottom. You'll wind up with a really sharp composition.

TIP
If you take pictures at an event, use them to tell the story of the day: when you arrived, who you met, and what happened.

135

Keep the **back-ground simple** so it does not distract from the subject.

If you shoot your picture **from below**, your subject will look menacing.

If you shoot **from above**, your subject will seem distant and insignificant

If you shoot your picture at **eye level**, it will look just right. Remember, this means the eye level of your subject, so if you are photographing animals or children, get down to their level.

TAKE TOP-NOTCH TRAVEL PICS

• Focus on **what you did**. Your snaps of your picnic lunch in Paris will be more memorable than the ones of famous monuments (besides, you can buy perfect postcard shots of those).

• If you do take a picture of a famous landmark, position your subject so you **follow their gaze** to the object in the distance.

• Make a **record of the journey**: snap family members packing, locking up the house, fishing for plane tickets in the airport, eating on the plane, then finally arriving at the resort.

Think: **Color**. Colors can either work together or they can clash. Make sure the tones in your composition are pleasing to the eye, and look for lots of nice contrast.

Use **natural shapes** and lines to emphasize your subject and draw your eye to it, the way this road draws your eye to the barn.

Look for **repetition** of shape, color, and line. These pencils make a neat composition since their shapes echo one another.

Don't think you always have to pose your subjects and make them say cheese! Sometimes the best photos are "**candids**," ones taken when your subjects are behaving naturally. Look for telling moments—when the birthday girl opens a present and gasps in surprise, when two players on a team high-five each other, or when your dad puts his arm around your little sis.

No one can guarantee your wishes will come true, but impeccable wishing techniques may help.

MAKE A WISH

YOU MAY *NOT* WISH FOR INFINITE WISHES. SORRY. NO CAN DO. NUH-UH.

On a Wishbone

★ Collect the wishbone from a chicken or turkey. Clean it off, then put in a warm, dry place for a day or two to let it dry out.

★ Have a friend grab one "handle" of the bone while you grab the other. Do not put a finger on the "head" of the bone to give yourself a better grip! This is cheating, and your wish will be rejected by the wish fairy. Your partner's wish will automatically jump into the "under consideration" queue.

★ At the count of three, each person makes a wish and pulls on the wishbone. When the wishbone snaps, examine both bits. The person who gets the larger piece of bone (the one with the "head" on it) will have his or her wish come true.

On a Star

★ Wait for a clear evening.

★ When you notice the first star in the sky, recite the following poem:

STAR LIGHT, STAR BRIGHT
FIRST STAR I SEE TONIGHT
I WISH I MAY, I WISH I MIGHT
HAVE MY WISH COME TRUE TONIGHT

★ Close your eyes.

★ Make your wish.

★ Don't tell anyone your wish!

On a Rainbow

When you see a rainbow, make the same wish three times. See if you can "catch" the rainbow in your hand. If you can, close your hand, make your wish, then "toss" the rainbow into the air to make the wish come true.

On a Dandelion

When you find a dandelion that has gone to seed, pick it, close your eyes, and make a wish. Blow off all the seeds in one blow. Watch as each seed carries your wish away to be granted.

MAKE SHADOW ANIMALS

Waiting for your wishes to come true? Here's a great way to pass the time. Try these inside a tent (with a flashlight) or on your bedroom wall.

Classic Bunny

The Flapdoodle

Swanee

Old Billy Goat Gruff

This Little Piggy

Hat Head

Bad Hair Day

#86

YOU NEVER KNOW

How to Prepare for a Space Mission #87

Congratulations! You've been selected to be the first kid to join a space mission. Here's what you will need to do to get ready before you leave for Planet Mergatroid.

but just in case...

1 Study hard and **get straight A's**. At astronaut training school you'll be given intensive classes on shuttle systems, math, geology, meteorology, guidance and navigation, oceanography, orbital dynamics, astronomy, physics, and materials processing.

2 **Get fit**. You will have to be strong enough to undergo rigorous survival training on land and sea.

3 Brush up on your **swimming skills**. Astronauts have to pass a swimming test during their first month of training. You'll have to swim three lengths of a 25 m (82 ft.) pool.

4 **Try climbing a mountain** or two. When you're at astronaut school, you will be tested to see how well you respond to high and low atmospheric pressures. A couple of days in altitude chambers will help you learn how to deal with emergencies associated with these conditions.

5 **Ride a rollercoaster** over and over again. This will help acclimate you to zero gravity. At the space school, you will get more experience with it by riding in a modified jet aircraft at speeds that produce 20-second periods of weightlessness. They also produce brief periods of an extreme desire to upchuck, so have your barf bag ready.

6 In your spare time, **get your pilot's license**. Before you can go into space you will have to demonstrate your flying proficiency by logging 15 hours per month in NASA's fleet of jets. You will also practice Orbiter landings in the Shuttle Training Aircraft.

7 **Practice living in tiny cramped spaces**. And get used to sleeping standing up. Astronauts never know which position their bed will be in at snooze time.

8 **Enjoy your meals** while you can. In space, you will be limited to dehydrated and freeze-dried meals.

When you have completed all of these steps, give yourself a pat on the back. You'll be ready to apply to the formal astronaut training program.

*N*ow here's a tried-and-true way to really wow your friends!

BLOW THE WORLD'S LARGEST BUBBLE

You'll Need

2 pieces of top quality bubblegum

1. Chew the gum well—about five to ten minutes. A perfectly prepared piece will have lost most of its sugary taste and be smooth and elastic, not too juicy.

2. Stretch the gum out by squeezing the blob between your tongue, the roof of your mouth, and the back of your top teeth a few times.

3. When the gum has reached the desired thinness, you are ready to blow. Curl your tongue so the tip touches the middle of the gum blob.

4. Push your tongue forward so that the front part of the gum blob stretches around the tip of your tongue.

5. Stick your tongue out, passing it through the opening between your lips. The gum should be stretched around and covering your tongue.

6. When your tongue is sticking about 1.25 cm (1/2 in.) out of your mouth, gently pull it back in, holding the bubble pouch in place gently with your lips.

7. With your tongue now out of the way, blow into the bubble pouch. If you are holding it firmly enough with your lips, it will catch the air and begin to expand.

8. Keep blowing, gently but firmly. Ta-dah! You have achieved bubbleness! Now it just takes practice to become the bubble king or queen.

Make Your Huge Bubble Pop!

- **Blow bubble as above.**

- **Do not seal off. Keep blowing, firmly.**

- **Bubble will pop with a loud explosion.**

- **See "Remove Bubblegum from Skin and Hair" (right).**

#89

MAKE A DOUBLE BUBBLE

1. Blow a large bubble.

2. Do not seal off.

#90

On Skin

Peel off.

Use another wad of gum to dab at the gum that's still stuck on your face. The face stuff will probably stick to the fresh wad, lifting off easily.

In Hair

Put four ice cubes in a plastic bag. Hold the bag against the gum. Break off the hardened chunks.

Or...heat a few tablespoons of vinegar. Massage into hair all around the gum. Shampoo out.

Or...plop a dollop of mayonnaise on and around the gum. Rub in. With luck, the gum will slide right off. Shampoo.

The largest bubble ever blown used Bubblicious gum. It measured 58 cm (23 in.) across.

3 There will still be a wad of gum inside your mouth. Following instructions for making a bubble above, flatten a portion of this wad and use it to blow a second bubble inside the first. Seal off both bubbles together. Ta-dah!

Who doesn't love to see shiny bubbles floating through the air? Now you can make your own.

MAKE A PRIMO BUBBLE SOLUTION

Recipe 1

The Simple Way. Add 15 mL (1 tbsp.) of liquid dish detergent to 250 mL (1 cup) of water.

Recipe 3

The Hard-Core Way. Combine 250 mL (1 cup) water with 15 mL (1 tbsp.) linseed oil (available from a health food store or a drugstore). Boil in a saucepan for five minutes until the mixture is light yellow. Let mixture cool. Add water to bring the total amount of mixture to 1 L (1 qt.). Add 60 mL (1/4 cup) liquid dish detergent. Let solution sit, uncovered, overnight before using.

Recipe 2

The Pro Way. Bubbles made with glycerine last longer. Combine 150 mL (2/3 cup) glycerine (available at a drugstore), 150 mL (2/3 cup) water, and 15 mL (1 tbsp.) liquid dish detergent.

MAKE A SQUARE BUBBLE

You'll Need

7 pipe cleaners

bubble solution

a deep bowl or tray

1 Bend 6 pipe cleaners to form right angles. Attach 2 to each other by attaching an end around a bend. Continue adding pipe cleaners to build a cube. Attach the last pipe cleaner to the cube to make a handle.

2 Pour enough bubble soluton into the tray so the solution can completely cover your cube-shaped bubble wand. Dip wand in to immerse.

3 Pull the wand out of the solution. A film will form on all six sides of the cube. If you are lucky, the films will draw together to form a square bubble in the center of the wand. Admire (don't blow on it or the bubble will pop).

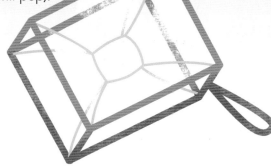

HOLD A BUBBLE IN YOUR HAND

1 Wet your hands thoroughly.

2 Blow a really big bubble.

3 Carefully catch the bubble with your wet hands. Don't let the bubble touch any dry skin or clothing. Ta-dah!

4 If you're careful, you can even stick your wet hand right *through* the bubble!

#93

145

#94

Y̶ou're coming up to an age where you go more places on your own and have more freedom. But if you're going to be out and about without an adult, then you've got to have safety savvy.

BE STREET SMART

TIP 1: Don't Leave Home Without It

Use this checklist below for the crucial pieces you should always carry with you:

Some ID. Of course you know your name, address, and phone number, but what if something happens and you can't tell anyone who you are? Always carry some identification with you.

The **name, address, and phone number** of someone you can contact if your parents are not at home.

Change or a phone card in case you need to make a call and don't have a cellphone.

TIP 2: Know Your Surroundings

• Scout out the neighborhood with an adult to identify any trouble spots you should avoid, and places where you can safely go if you feel threatened. Look for Block Parent houses, public places like libraries, schools, fire stations, houses of worship, community centers, and shops where you'd feel comfortable asking for help. Look for payphone locations too—you can always call 9-1-1 or a telephone operator at no charge.

TIP 3: Stay Alert

• Watch out for unusual behavior, like a gang of older kids following you, or a car keeping pace with you.

• Never, ever get into a stranger's vehicle—no matter how bad the weather, or how nice they seem.

• Never engage in conversation with a stranger who is driving a vehicle. Stay a safe distance away (out of arm's reach) and continue walking.

• If a stranger asks for help, be wary! Most trustworthy adults would not ask a child for help. Shake your head to indicate you can't help, and keep going.

TIP 4: Have a Plan

- Decide ahead of time what you will do if you or one of your friends is in trouble. Discuss the following scenarios with your friends, parents, teachers, and caregivers to develop your plan.

What should you do if...

- ...you get lost?
- ...other kids are pressuring you to do something you don't want to do?
- ...a strange adult approaches you?
- ...your expected ride does not arrive on time?
- ...you are being followed?

TIP 5: Take Positive Action

If, despite all your precautions, you find yourself in danger, ACT!

- Run! Put as much distance as possible between yourself and the problem.

- Immediately head to the nearest safe location. Tell an adult what happened right away. Don't wait to be asked, and don't worry about being polite. Interrupt, if you have to, to make your point.

- If someone grabs you, yell as loudly as you can for as long as you can until help arrives. Biting, kicking, rolling on the ground, thrashing about—all are perfectly acceptable ways to protect yourself.

BASIC RULE: SAY NO, GET AWAY, AND TELL SOMEONE.

ALONG THE WAY

- Stick to well-traveled streets. Avoid back alleys and empty lots at all times.

- Whenever possible, travel with a friend. If you are alone, stay on your guard! Walk in a purposeful manner, with your head up, eyes forward, hands free, and a brisk step.

- If you walk home from school every day, take the same route, and let your parents know the route you go.

- Steer clear of strangers. Never allow a stranger to touch you. Don't let a stranger lead you anywhere *under any circumstances.*

TIP 6: Don't Freak Yourself Out

Your chances of being injured or attacked in public are very small. The chances are even less if you are prepared. Go out and have fun! Your "streetproofing savvy" will kick in if needed. **147**

*I*t's fun to go to the mall with your friends. But sometimes, shopping can be overwhelming: salesclerks can be sniffy, price tags confusing, and prices sky high! Never fear, Teen Mall Queen Sally S. Hopper is here. She'll show you how to deal in Shopping Dos and Don'ts.

SHOP LIKE A PRO

Sally S. Hopper says:

• Puh-leeze—**don't act like a goof**. When you enter the store, behave appropriately. Talking loudly with your friends may disturb other customers.

• **Don't paw all of the merchandise**. If you mess up the displays, somebody like you who's working in the store will have to straighten them all out.

• In a lot of stores, a **salesclerk** will approach you and ask if they can be of help. Be polite. If you just want to browse, tell them so. If you are looking for a specific item, speak up. They can direct you right to the item, and even help you find your size.

SHOP AROUND FOR A GOOD DEAL

Many stores carry the same or similar merchandise, and sometimes the prices can vary a lot. To get the best deal on your purchase:

• **Visit two or three stores and compare items. Are they exactly the same (like a CD by your fave band), or slightly different (a shirt in two different patterns)?**

• Cheaper isn't always better. Yes, it's smarter to buy the cheaper CD, but a better quality shirt may be worth more if it lasts longer and wears better.

• Scan newspaper ads and flyers and wait for a sale if you can. Maybe you'll be able to afford two items instead of one!

GET THE RIGHT CHANGE

You're ready to buy. Bring all the items to the cash register. Make sure each item has a price tag attached.

DON'T RUSH! WHEN-EVER YOU'RE DEALING WITH MONEY, TAKE YOUR TIME. DON'T LET ANYONE HASSLE YOU OR MAKE YOU FEEL SILLY FOR BEING CAREFUL.

• Add up the prices for each item in your head and estimate how much your total, including sales tax, should be.

• When the cashier rings up your purchase, compare the total to your estimate. Is it close? Good. Then you have not been overcharged.

• Check the cash register receipt to be sure. Are all your items listed? Do the prices match the price tags? Look especially at sale items to make sure you were charged the lower price. Also check the quantities for each item.

• If you have exact change, use it to pay for your purchase.

• If you are paying with a bill larger than your purchase (say, $20.00 on a $14.23 purchase), the cashier will have to give you change.

• Calculate how much change you should be receiving. The cashier should count out the change to you out loud, like this:

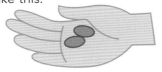

" 14.23...24...25..."

"50...75... 15.00."

"AND 5 MAKES   20.00. THANKS VERY MUCH!"

You should now have $5.77 in your hand.

• If the clerk does not count your change for you, take a few moments and check it yourself.

• If the change is less than you expected, triple-check it. If there is an error, politely point it out to the clerk. Wait for him to explain the bill so you under-stand it—maybe you misread something.

• Don't leave the cash register until you are sure you have received all of the items you purchased, at the correct price, and with the correct change returned. If a mistake was made, it will be tougher to get your money back later.

149

Why whistle? Because it's fun.
There is an art to whistling, and many different styles.
Here are instructions for the most popular types.

WET YOUR WHISTLE #97

The Classic Whistle

• Moisten your lips with your tongue.

• Purse your lips into an O. Leave just a tiny opening for air to squeak through.

• Place the tip of your tongue so that it lies just behind or on your bottom teeth.

• Blow gently. Did you get a sound? Great! If not, adjust your tongue position and the shape and position of your lips until you make a sound.

• Practice, practice, practice! Experiment by moving your tongue position to produce different notes. How hard you blow will make a difference too.

• You know you've got it when birds start checking you out.

On a Blade of Grass

• Find a tall blade of grass that is about a 0.5 cm (1/4 in.) wide, with a seam running down the middle. Pick it as close to the ground as possible.

• Smooth the blade of grass. Place it so the thickest part lies perfectly flat between your thumbs. Pull the blade up taut above with your pointer fingers.

• Do you see that little space between your thumbs right below your knuckles? Place your lips against it.

• Blow through the hole. Can you make the whistle? If not, adjust the grass and/or your lip position, and try again. If after a few tries, you still don't get it, choose another piece of grass and try again.

150

"Hail-a-Cab" Style

• Curl your lips over your teeth so that only the outer edges of your lips are visible.

• Choose any two fingers. The role of the fingers is to hold your lips in place over your teeth. Try any of these possibilities:

- a U-shape created with thumb and middle finger or thumb and index finger of either hand
- right and left pointers
- right and left middle fingers
- right and left pinkies

• Stick your fingers into your mouth up to about the first knuckle. Each finger should be about halfway between the corner of your mouth and the middle. Your finger-nails should be angled inwards, towards the center of the tongue.

• Draw back your tongue so that its tip almost touches the bottom of your mouth, about 1 cm (1/2 in.) behind the lower gums.

• Inhale deeply, then blow over the top of your tongue and lower lip. Press down with your fingers on your lower lip and teeth.

• Adjust the position of your fingers, lips, and tongue to find the "sweet spot"—the place where your whistle will have a strong, clear, and really ear-piercingly loud tone.

WHISTLING LIKE A CANARY

In the Canary Islands, people traditionally communicated over long distances with a language that was entirely made up of whistles! The whistling language, called Silbo, could be heard across distant valleys. It is still taught to children in schools throughout the islands.

Dazzle your friends! Impress your family! You can do these awesome magic tricks just about anywhere. The real secret is to never tell how you did them.

#98

DO A GREAT MAGIC TRICK

Ye Olde Disappearing Pencil Trick

You'll Need

a large handkerchief (or cloth napkin)

a pencil

1 Sitting at a table, hold the pencil up in front of you.

2 Say to your pals, "I bet you I can make this pencil disappear right before your eyes."

3 Cover the pencil with the handkerchief.

4 Say "Abracadabra!"

5 Remove the handkerchief, and voila! No pencil!

How Do You Do It?

When you drape the handkerchief, use your fingertip, not the pencil, to hold it up. To your audience, it will look like the pencil is still in place. But, secretly, you let the pencil drop into your lap so it's hidden between your legs.

TIP

The secret to all magic tricks is creating an illusion for your audience. Practice, practice, practice in front of the mirror because it's your performance that will really "sell" the magic.

Ye Olde Disappearing Penny Trick

You'll Need

a penny

a letter-sized (8 1/2 x 11 in.) piece of paper

1. Sitting at a table, hold up the penny in front of you.
2. Say to your pals, "I bet you I can make this penny disappear right before your eyes."
3. Fold the penny inside the paper.
4. Say "Abracadabra!"
5. Give the paper to your friends. When they unfold it, voila! No penny!

How Do You Do It?

When you fold the paper, do this:

First, fold the paper in thirds from top to bottom, like this:

Tip the paper up toward you to continue folding. Let the penny secretly drop out into your lap.

Keep folding the paper, as if nothing happened. It should end up as a square.

Of course when your friend unfolds the paper, there's no penny inside!

Ta-dah!

TIE AND UNTIE KNOTS

BASIC SLIP KNOT

This easy knot is essential for yo-yos.

1. Tie the end of the string into a loop. Knot it.

2. Push another piece of the string *through* the loop to form a second loop.

3. Slip your finger into the loop. Draw tail "A" tight. Notice how you can make the finger loop larger or smaller? The way the fastening slips back and forth gives this handy knot its name. It will hold fast over something solid, but will also come off easily, so it's a good choice for a very temporary fastening.

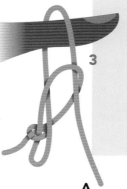

A

THE LARIAT LOOP

This is the knot cowpokes use for a lariat, or lasso.

1. Make a loop in the end of your rope, curving the short end *over* the long end.

2. Bring the short end up *behind and through* the loop. This will form another small loop next to the first. Hold this smaller loop open with your finger.

3. Stick the short end *around the outside* of the big loop, then *up through* the little loop.

4. Pull both loose ends, holding the larger loop until a knot forms. Your loop can slip larger or smaller to form the lariat.

FIGURE EIGHT KNOT

This knot forms an "8" shape when you are tying it. Use it to fasten two ends of string together, like when you are tying string around a package.

1. Line up the ends of the two strings and lay them side by side to make a double strand.

2. Make a loop with the end of the double strand, *crossing* the short end on top.

3. Make a second loop with the same end of the double strand to form a figure 8. This time, cross the loose end *under* the rope.

4. Poke the short end of the double strand *through* the first loop. Pull tight.

5. When you separate the strands, they will remain joined in a firm knot.

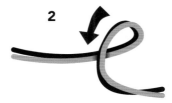

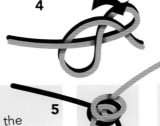

SAILOR'S KNOT

Use this reliable knot to attach fishing hooks to line.

1. Loop the end of the line around the hook.

2. Cross the line *under* itself, then poke the end *through* the loop that forms.

3. Keep the line slack, and repeat, this time crossing the line *over* itself and slipping the line into the second loop that forms.

4. Pull to tighten both loops at the same time.

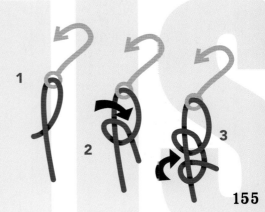

155

W e can't be happy *all* the time. But when you feel life is getting you down, try these mood-lifters to chase away a bad case of the crankies.

BEAT A BAD MOOD

Get outside for some fresh air and exercise. Exercise releases endorphins ("feel-good" chemicals from your brain) that elevate your mood. As a bonus, you can often work out solutions to problems while engaging in repetitive aerobic activities like running, cycling, or swimming.

Talk to a friend. Just sharing your troubles, or a laugh, will help you dump your dumps.

Do something nice for yourself. Take **time out just for you** and read, watch a favorite DVD, email a friend you haven't seen for a while, sort out your photos, play some music, anything that gives you a great escape.

Do something nice for **someone else**. This usually makes everyone happy!

Take a **warm bubble bath** and get a good night's sleep. You may feel like a new person in the morning.

Meditate. Find a comfortable place to sit quietly for a few minutes. Take several deep breaths, and try to think about nothing but the sound of your own breathing. A few minutes of meditation will help you calm down, and stay calmer for longer.

Are you tired? Take a **nap**. Sometimes just a few good minutes of shut-eye is all your body's asking you for and you'll find your mood will lift.

Are you hungry? **Eat** a healthy snack, like fruit. Or a small piece of chocolate. The chemicals in this tasty treat really do lift your mood.

Make time for fun. Laughing is one of the best stress-busters going. Giggle over your favorite book of comics, guffaw through a hilarious movie, or bust a gut with a best pal.

PUT IT IN PERSPECTIVE

Is it worry that's getting you down? Say, for example, that you are you worrying about a test. Ask yourself: What is the worst thing that can happen? Well, that you'll fail the test. And then what? Follow the chain of logical consequences. Chances are they really aren't so terrible. If you fail the test, for example, you might have to stay in after school for a few days to brush up on the material. In this case, worrying won't help—preparing will. Study extra hard before the test to improve your chance of success, and ask for help if you need it. Then just do your best. Sometimes, things really ARE that bad, and you might need to ask a parent, teacher, or guidance counsellor for help or advice.

Once you pick your joke, the rest is easy. Here's the stand-up comic's guide to getting giganto-laffs, every time.

TELL A JOKE #101

Knock. Knock.

Who's there?

Dwayne.

Dwayne Who?

Dwayne the bathtub!
I'm dwowning!

Did you laugh at this knock-knock joke? If so, then you already know the first rule of how to tell a joke. **Choose a funny one**. And choose a listener who will also think your material is funny.

Watch your pace. Don't speak too rapidly or too slowly—no one can laugh if they can't understand what you are saying.

Don't start telling the joke unless you are sure you **know it perfectly**— beginning, middle, and punchline. There's nothing worse than listening to someone start to tell a joke and then discovering they've told the punchline first, or that they can't remember the punchline.

Take time to breathe. No one wants you to expire before you get to the punchline.

Make silly faces for big laughs. A really great goofy face will take you far. Some of us are born with these. The rest of us will need to fake it. Try crossing your eyes, pursing your lips, or wagging your eyebrows. Add sound effects to really have 'em rolling in the aisles.

Timing's Everything

The way you space your words—that is, the pauses in between them—is crucial. You can call this your sense of timing. Timing is an art. Some of us have it, some of us are still learning it. To improve your timing, you'll have to practice. A lot.

Don't laugh at your own joke. That's the audience's job.

Think about how you would use timing to tell this joke: "What do you call a mom or dad you can see through? A trans-parent!" Would you pause after "through?" Would you take a beat after "A"? Would you stretch out "trans"? Try your joke out a few ways and gauge your best delivery by the loudest laughs from your audience.

Humor also comes from your posture and hand gestures. Use **expressive body language** to underscore the different parts of your joke and make it funnier. Are you telling a "Why did the chicken cross the road" joke? Fluff your (imaginary) feathers up and cock your head like a chicken. People will laugh even if your joke lays an egg.

Exaggerate. Either tell your joke in a wacky, super-dramatic style, or keep it really low key and deadpan. Contrast the joke itself with your delivery, and you'll score big laffs.

159

ANSWERS

Page 21 (Decipher Roman Numerals)

MMDCCLXVII is 2767. Still stumped? Here's how it breaks down: Each M is 1000, so MM is 2000. D is 500 and each C is 100, so DCC is 700 (500 + 200). L is 50 and X is 10, so LX is 60. And VII is 7 (5 for V + 1 for each I).

Page 30 (Keep a Secret)

Keep.
Keep.
Tell.
Tell.
Tell.
Tell.
Keep.

Page 84 (Choose a Pet)

1. If you answered C, choose an easy-care pet like fish, hermit crabs, gerbils, or certain reptiles. A few minutes a week is all that's required. If you answered B, consider a cat, hamster, or rabbit. They are low maintenance, but need to be fed daily, and cages and litterboxes will need to be changed regularly. If you chose A, consider a dog or ferret. Both need lots of attention, stimulation, and exercise. Birds also need very regular care, and cleaning of their cages must be done daily.

2. If you chose A, consider a dog, ferret, or white rat. If you chose B, consider hamsters, guinea pigs, rats, dogs, cats, or ferrets. If you are more interested in observing than playing with your pet (C), consider fish, some reptiles, gerbils, and degus. If you like a more exotic pet (D), consider snakes, hermit crabs, turtles, ferrets, or a tarantula.

3. If you chose A, think twice about getting birds, dogs, or cats. These species will be with you for many, many years. Instead, choose animals with shorter lifespans such as goldfish, gerbils, or hermit crabs. If you chose B, consider a traditional pet like a dog or cat. If you chose C, maybe a rabbit, guinea pig, or hamster is for you.

4. If you chose A, you can indulge your love of any type of pet. You need lots of space, in particular, for large breeds of dog or animals that have large cages like rabbits or ferrets. If you chose B, consider a smaller breed of dog, a cat, and animals with moderately sized cages such as smaller birds, hamsters, gerbils, rats, reptiles, and fish. If you don't have a lot of space, stick to smaller animals like rats, gerbils, hamsters, fish and hermit crabs.

5. If you chose A, stick to fish and gerbils. If you chose B, dogs and cats might be a good choice, but avoid smellier pals like birds (their cages get yucky quickly), hamsters, rabbits (P.U!) and ferrets. If you chose C, follow your nose to your favorite pet.

6. If you chose A, consider the original pet very carefully before introducing any new dogs or cats into your household. If you chose B, be wary of introducing birds, fish, or rodents (kitty snacks), dogs, or any new cats. If you chose C, consider whether or not you have time for any new pets! If you chose D, perhaps a pet is just what you need.

7. If you chose A, consider a non-furbearing pet such as a fish or reptile. Skinny pigs—specially bred guinea pigs with no hair—are also good choices. If B, then allergies don't need to figure into your decision.

Page 106-107 (Speak in Code)

Pig Latin phrase: "Pig Latin is easy." would be "Ig-pay atin-lay is-ay easy-ay." Ubbi-Dubbi phrase: "Whuby ubam Ubi spubendubing muby vubalubuubable tubime duboubing thubis crubazuby subecrubet lubangubuage thubing?" translates to "Why am I spending my valuable time doing this crazy secret language thing?"

Page 117 (Decode Text Messages)

Thanks: THX or TX
Mother over shoulder: MoS
How are you?: HRU
Great minds think alike: GMTA
I don't know: IDK
Yeah, yeah, sure, sure, whatever: YYSSW
You know what you could do: YKWYCD
Have fun: HF
What's up?: SUP
No way!: NW
Sorry, I got to run: SIG2R
Great!: GR8
Rolling my eyes: RME
Laugh out loud: LOL
That stinks!: PU
See you tomorrow: CU 2MORO
Hanging my head in shame: HHIS
Rolling on the floor laughing: ROFL
Don't think so: DTS
See you later, alligator!: L8R G8R
Sick of me yet?: SOMY
By the way: BTW
Where have you been?: WERV U BIN
Call you later: CUL8R
Best friend: BF
Bye for now: B4N
Just joking around: JJA

Page 119 (License Decoder)

VET DR: veterinarian
IISK8R: ice skater
QTPI: cutie pie
W8LIFTR: weightlifter
10SNE1: eager tennis player
8 2 MUCH: big eater
2BZ: person rushing
HIHO: one of the seven dwarves